FACTS & FICTION ABOUT PAST LIFE

A SIMPLE WAY TO KNOW PAST AND MAKE FUTURE BETTER.

DR. REKHAA KALE

Being a scientifically logical thinker, I never give any weightage to things that smell blind faith, baseless assumption, illusion, hearsay stories or imagination.

The famous statement made by a famous philosopher, Rene Decartes, "Dubito Ergo Sum & Cogito Ergo Sum" is the thing I always follow from the bottom of my heart!

Yet, when I am writing on the most disputed subject of past life, it is for sure, that I have had actual experiences of past life memories, not about just my own past life, but also about past lives of many others whom I helped to see through their past lives!

I dedicate this work to all those who helped me & motivated me to stay scientifically logical in the journey of subjects that easily attract imagination, illusion & blind faith!

Contents

Foreword ix

Preface xi

Acknowledgements xv

Prologue xvii

Introduction xix

LOGICAL EVIDENCE OF PAST LIFE

1. Logical Evidence 3

2. Evidences Of Past Life 5

3. Logical Tracing Of Past Life Memory 7

4. Real Examples Of Past Life Memory: 10

AURA

5. Aura 25

6. Meaning & Functions Of Aura 27

7. Presence Of Aura 30

8. Knowing, Touching & Seeing The Aura 32

DETAILS OF AURA

9. Details Of Aura 39

10. Formation Of An Astral Body 41

11. Levels Of Aura Of Living & Levels Of Aura After Death 43

12. Dissolving Of Astral Body & Problems In Dissolving It 47

13. Getting Ready To Be Born Again 51

TRACES OF PAST LIFE MEMORIES IN A PERSON

14. Traces Of Past Life Memories 55

15. Memory 56

16. Attitudes 57

17. Fears & Phobias 58

18. Inner Likes & Dislikes 64

19. Dreams, Desires, Drives & Fantasies 66

Contents

CONCEPTS AND THINGS RELATED TO PAST LIFE

20. Problems Arising Due To Past Life . . . 71

21. Concept Of Karma . . . 72

22. Obsessive Compulsive Rebirth . . . 74

23. Freedom From Obsessive Compulsive Rebirth . . . 75

24. Liberation = Freedom From Obsessive Compulsion . . . 76

25. Repeatedly Facing Some Situations . . . 79

26. Repeated Depressing Event Patterns . . . 81

27. Ailments Without Visible Cause . . . 83

28. Obsessive Compulsive Relationships . . . 85

29. Problems That Take Away All Energy . . . 86

30. Likes Or Dislikes Without Reason . . . 87

HEALING PAST LIFE TRAUMAS

31. Healing Past Life Traumas . . . 91

32. Past Life Traumas . . . 93

33. Knowing The Traces . . . 95

34. Getting Help Of A Master . . . 97

35. Remembering & Healing Trauma . . . 99

GETTING HELP FROM PAST LIFE MEMORIES

36. Getting Help From Past Life Memories . . . 103

37. Hidden Treasures In Past Life Memories . . . 104

38. Getting Help Of Healer To Find Hidden Treasures . . . 106

39. Using This Hidden Treasure In Present Life . . . 108

40. Developing Talents Brought From Past . . . 109

DEATH BARRIER

41. Death Barrier . . . 113

42. Knowing & Feeling Death Barrier . . . 114

43. Problems While Crossing Death Barrier . . . 115

Contents

SEEING PAST LIFE ON CROSSING DEATH BARRIER

44. Seeing Past Life On Crossing Death Barrier   119

45. Vision Of Past Life On Crossing Death Barrier   120

46. Future Ability To See Your Other Past Lives Alone   121

NEED OF A MASTER TO CROSS DEATH BARRIER

47. Need Of A Master To Cross Death Barrier   125

48. Effects Of Trying This Without Master   127

49. Risks In Trying To See Past Life Just By Reading Book   129

50. What Happens After Crossing Death Barrier   130

PAST LIFE VISION V/S IMAGINING & VISUALIZING

51. Past Life Vision V/s Imagining & Visualizing   133

52. Imagination   134

53. Visualization   135

54. Imagination & Visualization   136

55. Vision Of Past Life Memory   137

GETTING CLARITY IN YOUR VISION

56. Getting Clarity In Your Vision   141

57. Beginning To See   143

58. Seeing And Imagining   144

59. Imagination Free Seeing   145

60. Discarding Imaginations   146

61. Clarifying Our Own Vision   147

APPENDIX

62. Creative Visualization   151

63. Tips And Cautions In Past Life Healing   152

64. Creating Powerful Future After Healing Past Life   155

FOREWORD

Many people talk on past life. Many conduct courses on PLR, past life regression. Many claim to see past lives of others. But we rarely come across object approach in all these conversations.

Stories about past life are quite entertaining. But sometimes, they appear to be too amusing to be true.

This book not only gives you real stories about past lives they saw, but also tells how their present life issues got handles after seeing their past lives with this amazing technique.

This is because, seeing ast life is not enough, Correcting present life situations and handling present life challanges must be the real aim behind seeing past lives.

This book shows how to see the past lives in order to serve exactly this purpose and enrich our present life.

Preface

Past Life memories are memories of our past births.

Many do not believe in past birth. But, our own experience helps us to know that we did exist in past.

Past life is the life before the life we are living. Its traces are present in our system just like the bad sectors and soft wares without uninstall files are present on the Hard disk even after formatting. When the bad sectors are removed, hard disk is really cleaned.

Similarly, when past life memories are healed, present life is totally healed and one gets liberation from obsessive compulsive rebirths.

We claim to give logical explanation of every experience you get. We all know that every experience that gives us some kind of a shock leaves a deep impression on our mind.

If anything has hurt us badly or mortally, we fear it whenever we come across it again. This is a natural human and animal tendency. We also find that though we have never had any shocking experience about something, we still fear them, but, we are just not afraid of other things that may appear scary to others.

This fact is experienced by many. It certainly needs an explanation. When you cannot find the explanations of such fears and phobias, you have to accept that they have the roots in some of your past life.

You are still remembering the traumas you experienced in your past life. These fears and phobias are your gateways to your past life. Through them, you may look into the details of your past life, under right guidance of a master. We don't have just one past life as commonly believed. We have many of them.

Generally, it has been observed that the number of years a person lives; is the same amount of years he spends in astral form before all mental & emotional bodies dissolve and he is ready to enter new physical body. Then he is born again. This means, if a person had lived for 70 years, he will spend 70 years in astral form and then will be born again.

It is also seen that if a person commits a suicide, his aura has some aversion towards life, stored in it and as a result, he does not take birth in the above pattern. Instead, he spends 100 times the years he had lived, in this astral form before he is born again.

That means, if a person commits suicide at 20, he will be re-born only after 2000 years. This is the only reason why every religion considers committing a suicide a sin.

Even as the mental and emotional bodies are dissolving, the traumas and their memories still remain in minute forms that remain attached to the spiritual body. So when the person is born again, these memories get expressed as fears and phobias.

In some occasions, where the person does not want to die but has to leave the body force full, it is also seen that he does not wait for the period stated above. He then is seen to take birth almost immediately, usually in the same family.

At such times in some cases, you see that the people clearly remember their past life and that too in early childhood. As one grows, these memories fade away.

This means, logically, the past life memories that you may have would be of around 50 to 100 years before you were born. You may remember things even earlier to this.

One may go as back as 8 to 10 thousand years to see one's past lives and even see the details in that life clearly.

To be able to see the past life, you must first know the layers of your Aura clearly.

The Aura is supposed to have seven layers of which three are quite distinct. These layers are the physical, mental and emotional bodies.

Beyond them is the fourth layer that sort of marks the boundary. It is the spiritual body or soul.

The layers after these are not as clear as the first three.

These are, past emotional body as the fifth layer, past mental body as the sixth layer and past physical body as the seventh or the outermost layer.

The Aura is stretched and fixed around the physical body of a person, like an inverted rubber ball that has a thick inner layer and thinner outer layer, so, as the tension of inner layer starts increasing, the cut starts getting apart, and the ball bounces back to invert and get back to its original position with thinner inside and thicker outside layers. This happens when the end of a person comes near.

As the person is dying the Aura gets cut from the feet side and then inverts and forms a ball above the head.

Now the inner parts like physical, mental and emotional bodies become the outer layers of the ball that dissolve and become very thin before the person is ready for the next birth.

This ball leaves the body s the person dies and we say that the life has gone away from the body of that person.

The physical body is the part of the Aura that is just a few millimetres away from the physical body. After death, this is the first to dissolve. It takes about 10 days to 15 days for this to dissolve completely.

Then over one year, the mental body dissolves. But since emotions are very deep rooted and almost attached to the soul, they require almost as many years as the person lived to dissolve completely before the person develops a blank mental and emotional screen again as he takes a new birth.

Still, some traces of extremely deep rooted emotions remain. These take the form of phobias.

I remember I feared getting inside water for I was drowned to death some 5000 years back. This means in all the lives after that, I have continuously feared water and kept away from it.

Same kind of thing may happen to anyone. So, we must remember that the phobias are the gateways to our past life memories.

But of course, the memory has to be reawakened only under go through the whole experience of death once again as you are remembering that event that had caused death and trauma.

May be this is the reason why most of the people see the traumatic death. First as they see their past life.

We also must remember that unless we cross the death barrier, we cannot really look into our past lives. So if someone claims to show you the past life without letting you see or experience the death, be sure he is making a good fool of you!

To learn more about past life and solve your own daily life problems as well as other problems, contact author on rekhaa.kale@yahoo.com or on 9820044254 or 9870044254.

Acknowledgements

Past life is something that not all can logically accept, but on explaining the logical evidences about it, a large number of seekers choose to take up the past life healing sessions. There are many who talk about past life, but the validity of their visions is hardly crosschecked with the test of reality vs imagination check.

I urge all readers to understand the need of getting logical evidence of every experience they get, so that they can keep imginations and beliefs away from reality.

My students who were seeing past life with my help were all so co-operative that they could go through the reality vs imagination test for each of their vision and as a result, could conclusively understand that what they saw was actully their own real past life experience and that too where they could see the time period and location of the event with toatl clarity.

The very first time, when I was taken into my pasy life, it was done so casually, and it was only after I had seen and experienced the past life, I had realized that what I had seen was my past life.

I am really thankful to all my past life students who saw their past lives with my support, and those who took a teacher's training into taking others into past life and later permitted to share their experiences obviously with different names, here in this book.

Prologue

Past life is the life before the life we are living.

Its traces are present in our system just like the bad sectors and soft wares without uninstall files are present on the Hard disk even after formatting.

When the bad sectors are removed, hard disk is really cleaned.

Similarly, when the past life memories are healed, the present life is totally healed and one gets liberation from obsessive compulsive rebirths.

Introduction

Past life is the life we had before we took birth as we are just now. Some people say that we had 'A' past birth. This is not true. Each person has many past births. There are many past lives that we have had before we became what we are today. There is also a concept that person has only a human past life. This too is not true.

We are evolved from other animals. So, there are chances that in some of our past lives we were not humans. It is also believed that all cannot see past life. This too is not true. Practically all who can think can see and remember their past life. There are some religious and faith systems that do not subscribe to the concept of past life.

But this is only in order to protect the people from false beliefs and dogmas. With the logical evidence of it, even they accept that it is there.

Before you get acquainted to the past life, you must know that if you consciously see and feel some experiences that have not happened with you in this life, in this session, certainly, the memory is from your past life.

Also when you fear something that you have never even heard of earlier, and when this fear is almost a mortal fear, be sure that this fear has come from one of your past life experiences. May be, it was a cause of your death in that past life!

LOGICAL EVIDENCE OF PAST LIFE

- Logical evidence of past life
- Reasons for existence of past life
- Logical tracing of past life memory
- Real examples of remembering past life

I

Logical Evidence

Some take Past life as a myth while others take it as a blind belief. Some others say that it is a fact. The observation of actual events, memories as well as reactions can bring about logical evidences of past life. Anything that is not logical is not acceptable to a logical and analytical mind.

This is why those who talk of past life without logical foundation are ridiculed and disbelieved as cheaters by people of analytical mind. Very few know the existence of past life as a plain and simple truth.

The past life memories are inscribed in our life material in the form of images. One must never believe in whatever one hears about past life till the time one does not get a conclusive evidence.

One may be open for any logically conclusive evidence of past life to handle obstacles in this life. When a computer hard disk is moved from one machine into another machine, it needs formatting.

While formatting, all the data is removed from it, but bad sectors or softwares with no uninstall files, stay even after formatting. Same analogy applies to hard-disk of human life, called soul!

While transforming from one life to another, soul travels with layers that make the physical, mental, emotional energy bodies of living being. These are on each side of the soul.

While travelling from one life to another, memories are cleared as aura levels go through cleansing process. But the scratches of traumas and deeply rooted talents stay back.

These things touch the soul and create a mark.

So, After aura is cleared, the marks still stay and come back to next life as past life memories.

We find evidence of these sectors on soul in the form of phobias as well as inborn talents. They can also be seen by deep scientific introspection.

Some gifted kids are born with some talent. This gift comes from past life, when they had mastered that skill, when that life had ended while performing that task of excellence.

Some are mortally afraid of a few things without prior experience.

These are phobias caused by scratches of trauma on soul matter. They emerge from traumatic experience at the time of death.

Fears and phobias are carried from life to life as they are engraved in the life material.

The memory scars aura material keeps blocking ways during life after life.

But they get out effectively for good only after we remember the event that created this scar, by of systematic past life regression.

Then such event is brought back into memory & sent for dissolving by adding an un-install file to the memory file.

II
Evidences of past life

Past life is something that has been treated as true as life is said to be continuous. We all know that at birth, though a person welcomes life and enjoys it, there is only one truth of which he is always afraid. Yet he knows that that is the only truth in the midst of all the uncertainty of life. This truth is the death.

This means, if for a soul, death is inevitable after life, life also has to be inevitable after death!

There are people who say that by following spirituality, they can overcome birth & death cycle. May be, it is their opinion! But even in this statement, we come across a concept of cycle of birth & death. This means, there are many births and many deaths for every soul. But still many feel that there is nothing like past life.

Some say that their religion does not believe in it and so it is not there. Yet these people say that a person goes to GOD after death and God decides as to what to do to him after it! So, if God wants, he will be born again! Also, if GOD wants, he may stay with GOD for rest of the time.

But since no one has seen GOD or the origin of universe, all these things are taken to be just opinions.

We all know that the universe is vast. No one knows its origin or end. No one knows when it came into existence and when it will come to an end.

Most of the people are so busy in their daily struggle with life that they have no time even to think about the universe. But we all know that just everything has a beginning and end, even universe must be having some beginning and end.

In this universe, our planet earth is like a small particle of sand on the seashore! But on this planet too there are billions of living beings who are born and who die regularly. Now the question comes as to what is the beginning point & end point of life.

We may say that it is a soul that never dies as it is believed in many religious scripts, or we may say that just like red colour is created by mixing turmeric & lime juice when both of these are not red, life is created by mixing some elements in some proportion.

If we believe the later argument about creation of life, we cannot explain the phobias about some experiences that a person carries without having any previous experience or without hearing any previous conversation about such experiences. If we believe the former argument, we have to admit that there are many lives.

III

Logical tracing of past life memory

Everything that is scientific, can be objectively & logically proved. To accept that there IS something like PAST LIFE in a scientific manner, we must prove the presence of past life scientifically. Here is a small attempt to give logical evidences of past life that every individual carries with him.

We all know that no two persons are the same. Even identical twins brought up in the same surroundings show differences in many respects. The likes & dislikes, fears & phobias people have are not same in spite of same upbringing. Even their finger prints differ though they are born out of the same fertilised egg cell and share exactly the same DNA structure. This is certainly amazing!

It shows that though life making material is in exactly the same proportion while it is creating both the lives of these twins; there is still something that differs in both of them. This could be the soul! Every individual gets a different soul and every soul is covered with two sets of three layers of energy body, one set on each side of it. The inner set makes the physical body aura and the outer stays as past life aura around it and around the soul. These layers carry some memories. This is the reason why in spite of same heredity as well as same upbringing, identical twins have differences in interests and tendencies and attitudes.

The reaction pattern of a person is governed by his experiences as well as past memories. If one had good experience, one tends to like that thing, person, situation or place. People are comfortable with a thing or person or situation or place that makes them feel happy. If one had any bad experience about some thing, person, situation or place; one dislikes it. people feel restless even in the presence of such thing, person, situation or place that had given bad experience.

But some likes & dislikes we have about things or person or situation or place, are about things or person or situation or place we had never seen before. We know that all our emotions are learned by our experience so same must go even for likes, dislikes, fears, phobias and similar emotions. But some of these emotions do not show any memory in our memory line. If the likes and dislikes are based on memory or experience, how can such likes and dislikes come without experience or memory?

It indicates the pesence of some memory about things & experiences about which we have such unknown likes and dislikes. If these memories are not from this birth, they must be from past birth. Whatever we had experienced in past life is not known in this life, but reactions to those memories are imprinted in our soul. So, we have those reactions. This proves the presence of past life and of memories carried in it.

There are instances when we have some dreams repeatedly on certain occasions. We remember details of the dream quite vividly, and feel upset or happy just with memory of a dream, as if we are experiencing the actual event in real life. These have nothing to do with our life that we know, but we feel as if we know the things we see in the dream.

We feel that we know the places that we see in such dreams and feel that we have been regularly visiting or living in these places that we see in dreams. Also at times, when we visit some places, we feel some unknown familiarity for them though we have never been to those places. Sometime, on visiting some place, for the first time in life, we feel that we know the place and unknowingly start talking of some details of it that only the local people know!

Also, contrarily, on visiting some places, even for the first time in life, we feel unknown restlessness. We want to be out of that place at the earliest possible opportunity. At such times too we may find ourselves talking about some details of that place which one may never know without actually being there.

There are instances when one screams out of mortal fear on sight of some ordinary person or animal on seeing or meeting for first time in life. The person who reacts like this does not understand why he or she is reacting in this manner, but still cannot help such a strong as well as uncontrollable reaction.

Sometimes one meets someone for the first time in life, but both the persons who meet start interacting as if they know each other for years. They even end up asking and sharing many personal things that only good old friends share. Here we say that friendship clicked at first sight. But is it just that much?

Some situations give an unknown feeling of restlessness and we never know why that happens so often. We feel that this is a normal reaction to that situation, till we know from others, that we are over reacting. To others, those situations are just normal with no reason to generate anxiety.

May be all these reactions depend on some memories we have been carrying. What we get with life is the life material or aura. So we have to conclude that aura or life material carries memories from past life.

Some people ask if there is any example of a person who has never had any past life, and I will only say that since life is there on this planet for many many years, this is really a rare possibility. Every person remembers to have some likes, dislikes, fears, phobias, and feelings that have no traces in his present life.

These are traces of their past life memories. All have them. But all people do not recognise them clearly. This is the reason why people see their past life to know more about these memories more clearly. It helps us know as well as enrich our life.

IV

Real examples of past life memory:

Here I wish to share some experiences of people whom I have taken into past life during various past life healing training sessions.

All these experiences are real, but I have not disclosed the names of the persons to maintain the privacy of the individuals.

These experiences will tell you how a past life is seen and how one can handle the real life issues with this vision:

1: BURRIED ALIVE BY HUSBAND...

One lady was trying to see her past life for a long time, but was able to see only darkness.

Then, once, she introduced me with a boy she was planning marry. Later when she asked me how he was, I told her straight that she would be better off jumping from 10th floor instead of marrying that guy.

On asking I further told her that he is a guy who is a type who would have at least 10 affairs going at a time. She was shocked to know about my judgement, but confessed about two or three of them. Yet she was saying that he would improve after marriage.

Now I realised where she was getting stuck. Next time, when she was trying to see past life, I told her to clear the darkness with her hands. She found that it was like soil and sand.

She went on clearing it for nearly half an hour. After that, she saw the same guy whom she wanted to marry.

She saw that he was the husband of the girl she was seeing in the story. He had taken all the money of his wife and had buried her alive to go with her friend. By the way, that friend of hers in the past life was her friend even in this life, and this man already had an affair with her. This girl was well aware of that affair too.

When she was seeing this all, she did feel the suffocation as experienced during the process of crossing death barrier. On seeing all this, she realised why she was drawn to this man who even belonged to different religion.

She was still hopeful that he will improve. Now she realised that in that life, she had no chance, but life has given her a chance to change the pattern now. So, she must change it.

From next day, she stopped receiving calls by that person or meeting that person and now is happily married to her Mr. Right.

2: *KNOCKED DOWN BY A TRUCK...*

There was a girl who used to get scared to cross roads. Even while crossing a smallest by lane, she needed somebody to accompany her. She always used to fear that a truck will kill her.

When her mother was discussing this in the Reiki class, I explained to her, that this is due to the past life memories that the girl is having.

Later, I took that girl into past life.

Initially she was just creating stories about accidents she would imagine while crossing the road. But at one point, while telling the story, the girl almost screamed; "Oh no, that orange truck has killed me again!"

Next moment, she herself was shocked about what she said, but she actually felt that time that she was a 4 year old girl wearing white frock who was crossing the road in a hurry and an Orange Tata Truck of a model that was common about 50 years back, but now hardly seen, had run over her and she had died on the spot.

Once she realised that this was her past life and that now no such trucks are seen on roads any more, moreover, now she is grown up young lady and not a girl of 4 years, so she need not fear crossing the roads; her fear vanished.

3: PILOT WHOSE PLANE CRASHED...

A boy wanted to become a pilot since the age of 2. Now he was about 15.

He had come to learn Reiki to me.

That time, he spoke of all these things and then out of curiosity, wanted to see his past life.

He told about a dream of burning plain crashing in the sea; that he used to get from childhood.

I asked him to imagine the same and start with a story. He was just making storey and fooling with funny comments as well.

Then he said, ok since I have been seeing this burning plane, let me imagine that it crashed in the sea!

Because only that can happen to that plane!

As he started making a story on those lines, he saw that it was an air force plane.

Then he saw the burning plane crashed, but he was able to have an aerial view of it.

And he saw the search teams searching for the dead bodies. Then he saw a dead body being brought on the sea shore.

He saw some people gathered there and the dead body put in a coffin.

And suddenly this boy started crying bitterly.

I asked him why he was crying and he said, "But why is that lady crying?

I will take care of her, she is my wife, and doesn't she see me here?

I am here calling her, but she is just looking at my body and crying!"

Then he was even able to tell his name in that birth and the name of his wife.

After all that, he was able to understand his strong inner desire to get out of that burning plane alive and look after his wife who was all alone in the whole world!

This explained his dream that he used to get and the urge of becoming a pilot!

4: KILLED BY WATER...

Hydrophobia is fear of water. This is seen when a person is scared of water in any form whatsoever.

Some people are scared of water falling from the top, some are scared of sea or river water, some are scared of water collected on land like flooding.

All such fears come under hydrophobia. Some of them have a root in the present life experiences, while others have the roots in past life.

Here are a few cases of Hydrophobia:

4.1. Died due to waterfall...

There was a man who used to fear water falling on his head. He was not even able to stand under the shower in the bathroom, or put water on his head while taking bath.

He was not scared of river or sea, could also swim well, but could not tolerate water falling directly on his head. This appeared to be quite weird to his family, but no one was able to understand or explain this.

When he decided to see his past life, we chose the same fear and I asked him to create a story where the main character was threatened in some way by water falling on head.

On trying to probe into this fear he could see that while the character he had created was an archaeologist. He was working on many rare and buried monuments.

He would dig out the hidden and buried caves to find out about the lost civilizations in various different places around the world.

As a part of his research work, He was digging out some cave. This appeared to carry some important traces of some lost civilization.

When he was almost done, he was trying to come out of a cave in an unknown place.

Suddenly as he stepped out of the cave, he happened to come under a heavy waterfall due to some natural calamity and he had died due to that.

When he was seeing that the character in his story was falling like that, my student felt as if he was falling down after the water hit his head, and so, tried to restore his balance.

He then also felt that something hit his head strongly, and then he started seeing further part of the story as if he is seeing it while floating in air.

This was clear evidence that he had crossed the death barrier while seeing the character in his so called story, and that the fear he was carrying about water falling on his head had come from this life experience.

He was never able to tolerate water falling on his head as he was subconsciously remembering the past experience and after remembering it, he would fear that he would die now!

After seeing this past life his fear just vanished and then he started leading a normal life. Now he can stand under the shower without getting scared and can take a normal bath over his head.

4.2. Drowned when island sank...

This is my own experience when I saw my first ever past life.

At that time, I saw a lush green island with many golden langurs playing and jumping on trees.

It was a sunny day, but suddenly sky became cloudy, it started raining heavily, and also land started shaking badly.

Water of the sea started rising. The island ground was not seen as it was now covered by the sea water. Only the trees were seen.

Some langurs drowned, some were taken away by the force of water. Only those which were on the trees were safe and alive.

One of the langurs on the tree saw the tallest tree on the island and shifted to it. It went on going on the topmost branch.

It thought that come what may, this tree will be safe and so it will be safe too, moreover, as the branches are thick enough, he will be protected from rain as well.

But even that tree went under the rising water. This langur was neither able to come out nor save itself due to the thick branches above.

When I was seeing this, I started feeling a strong suffocation and in some time, the suffocation stopped and I felt very light.

Then, I tried to find out where this island was and when had this happened. It was some island near Australia, about 7000 years back.

5: SACRIFICED BY MASTER...

I was taking a person from some distance country in his past life over email chat. He had never visited India in his lifetime or known any Indian language. His issue was that he was always cheated or backstabbed by persons whom he trusted the most. He had taken a fear about trusting anyone.

In fact, he was wanting to handling this issue with the help of past life therapy. When he started creating the story in the process of his journey into his past life as per our process of past life healing method, he saw some place which he felt was a temple in Assam.

I asked him to check the pictures of that temple on net and tell me which image was similar to one he was seeing. He sent me a link of the image that was similar to the one he had seen during the process.

Then he told me that he was listening some chanting and said that it was probably in Sanskrit.

I asked him to tell me what he was hearing. But He hesitated to tell what he heard. He also said that he was feeling a fear in his mind as he is hearing the chants.

Initially he said that he was thinking whether those words he thought he was imagining to listen may or may not make sense, as he never knew any Indian language, and I told him that since I can read, write and speak Sanskrit.

When I still insisted, he said, that he was seeing some person who appears to be the master teacher of the boy he was seeing in the vision, and that that master was strictly insisting that he must not disclose those verses.

I told him that it is ok, as even the master is an imagination or vision as those words, so it does not matter and he need not listen to what the master in imagination is saying.

Then he started typing the words as he was hearing in his vision. He was not sure whether they would make any sense, but on my insistence, went on typing as he heard.

He also said that he was seeing the master annoyed and angry as he was typing those words. But later he said that the master had disappeared.

After that he saw that the boy, who was a disciple of that master, was offered as a human offering to some GOD by that master, so that the master may get some powers.

The person then realised why the master was earlier preventing him from telling the verses and seeing further.

When I checked for the actual meaning as well as authentic references about those words, I could make out that those words were actual mantras used in some worship procedures in olden days for sacrificing human being to God for achieving some deadly evil powers.

By the end of the vision, the person actually ended up in crossing the death barrier and realised that the boy he was seeing earlier, was he himself from his past life.

This means, he had seen that the person whom he was taking as his spiritual master had sacrificed him to God, for achieving some evil powers!

Now he could understand why, in the beginning of this Vision, it was the same master who was preventing this person from speaking out the Sanskrit verses chanted at that time.

Then he realised that after the spiritual master he had trusted the most and had left his house for, had backstabbed him in this manner, he went on getting into the trap of being backstabbed by people he would trust, and this was continuing even now!

On realising this, he started seeing the ways in which he could prevent it, and now, he is out of this vicious circle where, anyone he would trust would cheat him!

This was a really unusual and sad experience as it clearly revealed the presence of some practices that no one may even imagine to be true.

More so, the vision was experienced by a person who has had no relation with India or any Indian language, one has no way to even suspect that it might be his imagination, especially when the Sanskrit verses he had typed did tally the actual scripts meant for the said purpose.

I was sadly shocked to find that such things were actually there in India about 700 years back.

6. BULLET IN THE KNEE...

A person suddenly developed severe knee pain at the age of 27. He had no history of any knee or joint problems. He had never had any accident or had fallen any time. There was no joint pain history in his family.

He underwent all possible tests and found that all tests were normal. Doctors tried to give many medicines for stopping the pain but nothing worked, instead, he got side effects of those medicines, so doctors advised him to stop them.

Then he came to me. I could see this as a case of past life issue carried forward in this life, so I suggested him to go to past life with this issue.

After I explained him the details, when we started with actual regression by using our story method, he saw that a soldier was standing near a cliff as the war was on, and when he was attacking the enemy soldiers with his gun, he was shot in his knee, and as he bent with the severe pain due to the injury, he had lost his balance and had fallen down in the valley, and that was his end.

As he was seeing this all, he was experiencing the bullet hit, severe pain as well as the suffocation due to fear when he was falling in the valley.

This all showed that he had crossed the death barrier during this vision.

It means, he had seen his own past life after he had started with the story of the soldier. When all this had happened, the soldier in the story of my patient was also 27 years old.

My patient, who had developed this sudden pain in the knee, was also working on some situation of life and death importance, when he got sick with this sudden knee pain.

The situation he was working on was no different than war; the only difference was that this war was on a different plane.

So he realised that when he encountered similar situation in the present life, at around the same age, he was hit by the invisible bullet that was the cause of his death indirectly in the past.

Surprisingly, after that past life was seen and he realised that it was the bullet that had entered his knee in the past life, and now, it was causing the pain in this life; his pain vanished as if a miracle had happened, and later for past 10 years, he has never had any knee problems.

7. BITTEN BY SNAKE...

Ophidiophobia or Snake phobia is strong irresistible fear of snakes. This is one of the many phobias seen in people and reported by psychiatrists.

This is seen in people either after encountering real snakes sometimes, or when one has had a death by snake bite in the past life.

Such phobias may be so strong that a person cannot even see a snake on screen.

Here are a few instances when people have handled this phobia on seeing past life.

7.1. Eggs stolen by snake...

A young man who was about 28, had approached me for seeing his past life.

He had a very poor vision, but he was not having any problems about his vision.

His problem was that he was scared to get married, as he feared that after he gets a child, a snake will eat away his child.

This fear was so strong that he was strongly opposed to getting married.

Still his parents had not given up hope.

But whenever his parents would come across a proposal and introduce him to the girl, everytime, he would ask that girl if she knows how to handle a snake, especially if that snake comes and starts taking away their baby.

The girl as well as her family would find this question quite odd and would think that the boy had some psychological problem.

His parents were extremely worried about the situation and did not know how to handle this fear of their only son.

More so, the boy was not even interested in handling his eye problem. He said that no one can do anything about his eyesight.

Surprisingly, the young man who would ask this way about snakes had never seen any real actual snake in his lifetime till that time.

So, I decided to take him into past life to resolve this issue.

He saw a pair of ostriches. Of them, the male was hatching the eggs in the evening, while the female was out to fetch food.

A snake came there and tried to eat away the eggs. The ostrich first could not see the snake due to his poor sight, but when he saw, he tried to fight out the snake, and the snake bit him.

The ostrich died due to the poisonous bite of the snake. Later the snake took away the eggs and the ostrich could not do anything as it was dead.

But while seeing this, the boy was weeping and saying that now he can see the whole view as if from high in air. He also felt a pain near his eye when the snake bit the ostrich near his eye.

Also he experienced the burning and pain in the whole body as he was seeing the ostrich die out of the poisonous bite of that snake.

All this proved that he was seeing himself when he was seeing the ostrich.

After seeing this, both, his eyesight improved and his fear about marriage and snake taking away the child went away!

7.2. Snake bite in water...

A lady who wanted to see her past life said that she cannot put her feet in water. She is scared. Even when she would go to any beach, she would never let her feet touch the sea water.

Her fear was that a snake will bite her feet and she will die due to that.

Surprisingly, she had seen snakes only in movies and never in real life.

This means, her fear was certainly from her past life. So, I started probing in it. While creating a story, she saw a young girl who was sitting on the shore of a river, somewhere in north India.

She had her feet in the river water and was enjoying the touch of cold water of river.

Suddenly, this girl felt the cold touch of something slippery, smooth and long. Before she could see what it was or withdraw her feet from water, she felt some bite and severe pain.

Before she could even express her pain, she started feeling suffocation and she fainted.

Her friends took her out of there and tried to call for help, but by the time her family arrived, the girl was dead.

It was concluded that she had died due to the bite of some very poisonous snake from the river water.

As this lady was seeing all this in her story, she felt the suffocation when the girl in her story was getting suffocated.

Then, when the friends were taking her out from there, she started seeing all the things happening as if she is up in the air and watching the events.

Then I explained her that actually, the girl she was seeing was her own past life, and that when she saw the snake bite, she was remembering what had happened with her in that life.

This is the reason why, she crossed the death barrier while seeing the snake bite.

After she had left her body, the vision shifted from ground level to aerial level, as her soul that was seeing all the further events was actually up in the sky, floating around her body.

8. BURRIED ALIVE…

This is a common cause of claustrophobia as per my observation.

One of my students used to feel suffocated in any closed place. This was happening to her from her childhood and she had never known why this happens, but as a result, she was always keeping away from closed places. She would even avoid travelling in lifts that were totally closed.

I started taking her into past life and she started creating a story as per my method.

In her story, when she was just imagining some character at random, as per my method, suddenly, she saw a young girl of about 11 years forcibly captured and taken by force by some soldiers, who tied her hands and dumped her in a pit. Then they had mud and soil put in that pit which made the girl get totally buried.

As she was seeing this, she started getting suffocated and breathless. She felt as if she is dying, and asked me if she should stop the process. But I asked her to continue. I also told her that at a right time, I will ask her to stop.

She continued. Now she saw that even when the girl was under the soil, she was seeing the soldiers who had buried her, from some height above them. She wanted to punish them for what they had done, but was feeling helpless. She asked me if she could do anything about this.

Then she told that she was always feeling angry with soldiers wearing any British uniform whenever she would see them even in movies.

I asked her about some more details of the girl and the period when this had happened. She told me about those things and it showed that it had happened in the British period when the British tyranny was at its peak.

She was about to get into more details, but I interrupted as seeing them in her case was likely to create feeling of dual personality. She was from a much better off family in that life, so she could start comparing that life details with her present life, and that could cause problem, so I stopped her and told her not to get into details that may conflict with her present life.

This too is very necessary while seeing a past life. We must know where to stop. Else, we may start thinking about the past life we like and get disturbed in this life.

9. FELL DOWN FROM CLIFF..

Acrophobia or Fear of heights seen in many have a similar root cause as this experience instills a deep fear of height as the person is leaving his body either while falling down or after he hits the ground after falling down from great height. Many people fear heights, they do not like to look down from great heights and cliffs. But this becomes a problem when one has it even near an enclosed window of a higher floor of a multi storied building.

9.1. Fell from mom's hands...

A Reiki student of mine was willing to learn past life healing. She was going through her regression session.

That time, while talking of various fears and phobias, she said that she feels restless when she stands near the window of her house. She was staying on the 15th floor.

So she started making a story of someone walking up hill. As she was proceeding, first she started with some girl's story.

This girl in her story was about 6 years old, but as she went on making the story, suddenly she saw a small baby being carried by her mother.

Then she saw that the mother heard the voice of some wild animal, something like a tiger's roar, and she was scared. At this time, the mother was near some cliff on the hill, and in the effort of looking back, she slipped from the cliff. Both the mother and the baby fell down from the cliff.

This lady saw this, and started feeling breathless with the vision. Then whatever she started seeing was as if she is seeing from somewhere up in air.

She saw the mother trying to hold on to a stone and trying to come up, she also saw the baby down in the valley. Then she saw the mom weeping for her baby. She also saw the villagers going down and getting the body of the baby.

Now after explanation and analysis of her experience, my student realized that she was that small baby who had fallen from the cliff.

After this vision, my student found that she was comfortably able to look down from her window, from her apartment that was on 15th floor.

9.2. Fallen during trek..

Another student of mine was also scared of heights. He was also interesting in treks, but would avoid cliffs and valleys while trekking.

When he started with his story, he saw a boy about 21 years who was trekking with his friends in some place in North America. The friends were joking and climbing.

This boy was walking with a friend with whom he had some argument during this walk. The boy was a bit abusive and his friend tried to hit him for the abuse. In this process, this 21 year boy slipped from a rock and fell down the valley.

When my student was seeing this, he felt the falling and then suddenly he said that his view of the event had shifted from ground level to air level.

Later he saw the way in which the friends went down the valley, got the 21 year old boy up. The friend who was fighting with him was weeping & giving first aid thinking that he was unconscious. He saw that these friends took him to a hospital, in a car, where he was declared dead.

After this vision he stopped getting scared of heights any more and now is trekking without fear.

AURA

- Aura

- Meaning & functions of aura

- Knowing the Presence of aura

- Touching the aura

- Seeing of the aura

V

Aura

Aura is the energy body of a person that appears as an electromagnetic etheric energy field around the body of a person. In still simple language, we can say that Aura is the atmosphere around a person.

Some people use Kirilian camera to photograph it, but just as the gases in atmosphere keep changing every moment, the colours in our aura too keep changing every moment as per our thoughts and moods.

One can touch the aura with hands. On training, one can even see it with eyes under normal conditions and develop this vision further with regular practice.

Any one can easily learn to touch aura that is, this etheric energy field with hands and know about its condition just from the feel of it at any particular area around the body. Some people are born Clairvoyance. These people can see the aura just with open eyes without any special training.

Every living and non-living being & thing has an Aura around it. The quality and thickness of this aura is different from person to person and thing to thing.

If Auras of two persons or things or a person and a thing, blend with each other well, they get along well.

In the training of aura reading, one can learn all the scientific things about Aura that can be conclusively proved.

When one learns aura reading, one learns to feel the Aura of anyone or anything anywhere with hands. With the aura reading attunement, one can see the Aura with your eyes closed as well as open. After this training, one can easily learn to heal the Aura just by using ones thoughts.

During the aura training, one learns to find out the good and bad areas in the Aura. One also learns that he has to heal only the bad areas not the good ones. When all this learned, one can do wonder healing just while casually by talking to your patient.

When one is seeing the past life, one has to know some basic things about aura. On knowing these things about aura, one can know in which part of our aura we have stored the said thoughts and emotions from past, that are blocking our present, and then we can easily search for the memory and get free from the ties of our past.

VI
Meaning & Functions of Aura

Meaning:

We feel the presence of Aura by bringing any object near us at around 4 to 6 inches distance and feel the presence of that object by feeling the mild touch or pressure or hot or cold or just moving air as the object is brought closer. We stop feeling thi8s different feeling as soon as the object is taken away. Anyone who wants to test can try this and feel the presence of aura by himself.

We all know about lines of force around a magnet. They are seen as we place iron powder spread over a piece of paper. Place a magnet on a paper and tap the paper lightly. On doing this, we can find that the particles or iron powder get arranged in a certain way forming some curved lines in a particular order. These indicate the lines of force of a magnet that represent the energy around it.

Similarly, we find lines of force around electrically charged objects. The lines of force seen around electrically charged objects are also almost the same as the lines of force around a magnet.

We have the capacity to sense these lines of force and the feeling we saw above is due to exactly the same. It's due to this energy field that at times, even before we touch object having energy field, we get a shock.

Aura is the energy field around us. The only difference is that it does not just contain energies, but also has some matter in it. This matter is in plasma state. It has layers that differ in thickness.

We can feel the touch of this aura around any person from a reasonable distance. This is the reason why if you are walking and someone is just walking behind you for a reasonably long time, even if you don't hear his footsteps or you don't see shadow of that person you tend to look back to know who he is. You feel the presence when the aura of that person touches your Aura.

In this way there can be many evidences that make you know the presence of Aura in daily life. May be you must have felt it, but may be you have never realised that it is the feel of the aura.

Also you may find that you feel comfortable in some Auras while you do not feel comfortable in some other Auras then you say that the presence of someone makes you happy while you do not like the presence of someone.

This is just attraction or repulsion of auras. When auras blend with each other, we feel attracted to the person who has that aura, and when auras repel, we dislike the person who has that aura. So at times, when we meet someone for the first time, we just like or dislike that person.

This means, atmosphere around us that is charged with energy, is aura. It speaks volumes of our past, present, health & personality. We can see touch and change it if we know how to do so. This can not only heal a person, but also can remove dense energy blocks in it thereby releasing a person of many problems.

Functions:

Aura is the atmosphere around a person. This means, our body receives and gives away energies through this aura, in short, though we breathe with our nose, our energies breath through our aura. It prevents the energies to enter directly into the body of any person.

Yet the energies enter the aura and as per the resistance level of aura at certain points, they slowly go on penetrating the aura.

So, the aura has a protection shield over every entry point from where the energies enter the human body. This shield is like net that prevents thick dense energies from entering the body.

Aura is the etheric layer around us made up of plasma through which the inflow and out flow of energies happen. The light energies are life energies that are good to keep the body healthy. The dense energies are the death energies that cause the decay in the body.

So, aura accepts the light bright energies and gives out the dense dark energies. This process is just like our breathing where body takes oxygen and gives out carbon-dioxide and other harmful gases created during digestion of foods. Aura breathes energy for body and soul.

It protects our body from dense energies that can cause ailments; it pulls good energies towards us with its attraction and repels away bad energies with its repulsion.

VII
Presence of Aura

Some think and say that only gifted people can see or feel the aura. Some others say that those who reach some spiritual excellence can see the aura. Some say that very hard and rigorous meditations are needed to get the Siddhi of aura vision.

Some say that one must be gifted in order to be able to see the aura. Some say that people belonging to dev gan and rakshas gan can see the aura but not the ones belonging to dev gana.

But these are myths. Aura is a simple reality and anyone who wants to feel or see it can do so. Anyone can feel presence of aura around himself with just a little bit of training.

This means, knowing about aura is just a matter of keeping your antennas open while doing your daily routine things! This means it is just a matter of watching daily experiences with awareness.

It helps us to know the presence of aura around us very clearly. Once we know the presence of our aura so well, we can know many things about ourselves as well as others with that knowledge.

While walking in sunlight, have you noticed your shadow? Did you notice that your shadow gets hazy at the end and the line of demarcation between your body and rest of the area is not sharp in your shadow?

Have you found that the edges and sides that are seen on sides of our shadow are not as sharp as edges of shadows of things or buildings?

Have you noticed this difference between the shadows of living and non living beings? The shadow of living beings does not have sharp edges as the shadow of any other object.

Its sides go on being lighter and we cannot see a sharp line discriminating a shadow and the rest of the area around the living being as we can for shadow of any other object.

The decreasing luminosity of light near the edge of shadow of a living body indicates the presence of some matter outside the body through which light can pass partially while through rest of body light cannot pass at all.

This partially transparent matter can be called as translucent. This means it is not fully opaque as the physical body, but also not as totally transparent as clear glass or air.

This matter around the body of a living being is likely to contain something that is thinner than solid or liquid, but thicker than gas. Matter in such state is called plasma. This is a reason why many say that aura or life matter is made up of plasma.

We can even find magnetic deflection in this area at some points. May be we can experiment on the shadows by creating various magnetic fields around a person and study the difference in the shadow.

The experiments will show difference in the thickness of the hazy areas around a person's shadow. This means the matter that makes an aura, has magnetic property as well.

VIII

Knowing, Touching & Seeing the Aura

Knowing the Aura

We can know the aura of any person or animal by touching it, or by seeing it.

We have seen above that anyone who wants to see the aura can learn to do so.

This can happen either by birth or by proper scientific training.

A right training can enable any person of any age and educational background to see or touch aura.

Still there are some who do not want to trust their capability.

They are ready to spend huge amounts to do things that will prove that they are incapable of having some such ability.

So, those who say that they cannot see or feel the aura and cannot learn to do so, can even see the Kirilian photographs of aura that will photograph your aura at some one time; by spending the same amount in which they can learn to see or feel the aura for their life.

Aura has different colours and thickness. This is evident all around and more specifically at chakras around a person.

Its colours and thickness keeps changing just as the gases in the atmosphere keep changing in quality and quality every time. These qualities change with thoughts as well as health conditions.

The aura condition determines the health condition of chakra and in turn health condition of the person. To know the aura, we need to know how to touch it or see it.

This can be done by taking up the trainings that help us to see or touch or know about aura in right way.

If one wants, one can spend big amount and have the Kirilian photo taken.

But photo may show the aura only at a particular time and the aura colours keep changing as per the mood and spiritual condition of a person.

The aura conditions around a person are exactly like the gases in the earth atmosphere keep changing as per the circumstances.

So we must watch the aura for a reasonable time to know which colours are permanent and which colours are transitory.

The wrong permanent colours in the aura of a person need healing while transitory ones get healed on their own.

When we know the aura, we can know about many things about the health as well as the mind of a person. Then we can predict things and correct them too if needed.

Those who have learned Reiki till level 3 from qualified Teacher know how to scan the aura by touch.

The Pranik healing practitioners can know how to touch the aura by hands and heal it by touch.

Also, an Aura healing student can know how to see as well as touch the aura.

In all these healing methods, the teacher teaches how to differentiate between densities developed in this life and the ones developed in past lives.

One can feel this difference by the thickness and feel the quality of the energy matter by its feel.

This will help you to know of your past life karmas.

Touching the Aura

To touch the aura with hands, we must know how to make our hands sensitive. For this, lightly press centres of palm with thumbs. Then press fingertips against each other for a while. Now move both hands clockwise and anti-clockwise keeping the palms facing each other and keeping them at about 6 inches away from each other. On doing this, in a few seconds, we start feeling some different sensation in palms.

Now try to increase and decrease distance between palms. Watch the difference in sensation. When the sensation continues, try to bring one hand slowly at about 2 to 3 inches distance near any part of body. Try to see the feeling on palms.

We have same kind of sensation on our hand at some level near our body. This is the feeling of touch of the Aura. You get the same as we touch any other person's Aura too.

One may try to learn touching the aura just by reading this part of this book, but ideally, taking a proper training of the same during past life healing or Reiki or Pranik healing or Aura healing class is advisable. In such a class one learns this technique perfectly under able guidance.

When we master the art of touching the aura and practice it for reasonably long time, we can also learn to differentiate between various sensations received by our palm. This enables us to know the difference between good and bad energy. Then we can say where dense patches are located.

Seeing the Aura

There are few people who can see Aura right from birth. But percentage of such people is very less. Others can see it with proper training, practice and initiation for it from a master.

When we try to see the Aura, we need to concentrate on the background around the body. As we do this, we can slowly start seeing a thin layer of some colour due to which the background till around 6 inches away from a person looks different than the rest of the background. If the background is plain we get clearer vision of Aura.

This is the Aura of the person. One may or may not be able to see it just like that without proper training. Some persons can see this right from birth, but others cannot. They need training and attunement of aura reading. Then the aura vision of the persons who learn aura reading gets clearer. But it is certain that all can see the Aura.

After you start seeing the aura, you can also find out about the health condition of a person just by looking at him. This is because the aura of a person speaks of his health condition.

If a person is having some problems anywhere in the body, you can see some dark greyish colours in that area around the body. These dark areas are the dense energies around a person.

When the energies increase in density, they start preventing a smooth transfer of energies around a person and as a result that part of the body starts getting sick.

Also, when there is some past life memory in a particular area of a person, there is a thick dark spot seen in aura and this can be released only by releasing the past life memory of that person.

Those who can see aura or study aura by its feel can differentiate clearly between the dense areas developed in this life and brought from past life.

This is because the areas brought from past life are much denser and stickier than the ones developed in this life.

Any Reiki 3 healer, that is traditionally called as a Reiki master, who has learned this level of Reiki from a properly qualified Reiki teacher, learns scanning of aura at this level.

Then he can certainly know how to find out this difference.

Any person who has learned even basic Pranik Healing can know how to scan the aura with hands and spot the problem areas.

He also learns how to differentiate between lightly dense and strongly dense energy blocks around a person.

Any person who knows how to read the shadows that fall in proper sun light scientifically, may be able to see the denser areas in the shadow around a person and judge that that is the area where hi9s past life problem lies.

Also, as one starts growing spiritually, this Aura vision starts getting clearer and clearer.

Initially one may try to close the eyes and try to visualize the Aura around a person.

This will help you to see at least some part of the aura.

DETAILS OF AURA

- Details of aura

- Levels of Aura of Living

- Levels of aura after death

- Formation of an Astral body

- Dissolving of the Astral Bodies

- Problems in dissolving astral bodies

IX
Details of Aura

Aura around a person or animal has a number of layers.

It is believed that there are 7 layers of aura.

But I would say that there are 10 layers, of which, 7 stay as well as go with the body, while the other 4 are created by the thoughts about the person or animal in the minds of various people around.

So these 3 layers stay even after the death of the person or animal.

This is why may be after death of any big person or celebrity, during the final procession, people say, 'long live ---- (that person)'

The layers of aura are determined by the difference in density of plasma matter that makes the aura of a person.

The layers that are closer to body, this matter is denser.

So these layers are clearly visible or touchable.

But as the layers go away from body, the density of plasma matter goes on reducing, so their visibility and tangibility reduces.

This is exactly like atmosphere and its density around earth.

As we go away from the sea level, the density of atmosphere reduces and air becomes thinner!

As per density difference, we can differentiate between different layers of aura around anyone.

When a person is about to die, this aura starts leaving his body.

As a result, we find that aura from feet onwards starts getting out of body.

It starts leaving the body right from lower loimbs to higher.

Approximately 72 hours after the splitting of the aura starts, the aura separates from whole body. Then, it gathers and forms a ball above the crown chakra of a person.

The aura then reverses and forms a ball of aura above crown chakra, in inverted manner, with just opposite layers with outermost layer of living as innermost layer.

These layers dissolve slowly as time passes.

The density of first 7 layers of our aura is determined by the spiritual power of a person while the other 3 layers, i.e. the 8-9-10th layers depend on what people think about the person.

May be that is why we can say that the auras of people like Einstein or Newton or Shivaji Maharaj or Gandhiji or any such person wo is still remembered by people of today, is still existing!

This exists as long as that person will be remembered by people.

This is why it is said that a person lives through his good deeds even after his death!

X

Formation of an Astral body

Astral body is the energy body of a person outside his physical body.

When it surrounds the physical body, it is called aura, and when it is outside physical body, it is called astral body.

So actually aura & astral body are names of same body around us.

When any person goes on an astral travel, knowingly or unknowingly, while alive, similar astral body is formed. This is formed both when a person is living and when a person dies.

But, when a person is living, this comes back and settles as aura after astral travel, while, after death, it does settle around a person again.

It starts its journey ahead! In a living person, this astral body is connected to the body through a cord from the crown chakra.

This is the reason why it can get around the person again after the astral travel.

But at death, this cord is cut and the astral body is separated from the physical body.

So, the energy body of a person who is dead cannot get stretched and placed around the physical body of a person again.

In astral body, the order of aura layers is just the reverse of the actual aura layers.

This is because this time, the aura breaks from the feet and then gathers above the crown as a ball. This ball then moves out of the body.

Generally size of this ball is as small as table tennis ball.

So, when we go are astral travel, we are just about one inch in height.

If this happens in a living person, the chord that joins the astral body to physical body gets stretched.

So, there is a possibility to get attacked by other auras that have left body and are searching for a body to be in.

So, when one is trying astral travel, the first thing one must learn is to protect this connection of the astral body with the crown chakra.

If one fails to do so, and if some accident happens at astral plane, the astral travel may be fatal!

As the energy body leaves the body at death, and astral body is formed. This floats in the air like a balloon.

At death this is formed. This time balloon is formed finally, without capacity to get reversed to original position.

When astral body is formed at death, it has 7 layers as well.

The central layer i.e. the fourth layer is the soul or spiritual body as in the aura of the living, but here, the layers are reverse. The outermost layer of the aura of the living is now the innermost layer.

This is the layer from which in future the new physical body is generated. Then this layer becomes the physical body layer of this new born person.

This astral body floats and travels around till all the baggage from it is dissolved and till it is cleared.

XI

Levels of Aura of Living & Levels of Aura after death

Levels of Aura of Living

The Aura has 7 levels or layers. They can be distinguished by way of their thickness. We can touch and feel this thickness difference.

The first three are thicker and so can be more easily felt. The first level of Aura is just a few millimetres away from the body. This is the thickest level of Aura and appears as shining bright line of white light to those who can see Aura. This is the physical level of Aura. It indicates energies in our physical body.

Then we find the second level of Aura that is about 4 to 6 inches away from the body. It is this level that one touches when Aura. This level of Aura is thinner than the first level. Yet it is thicker than the other levels. This is the emotional body. It stores all the emotions that have an impact on our physical body as well as that create some of our experiences too. The emotions here are based on our past experiences of this and past life.

Then we find the third level of Aura. This is around 8 to 10 inches in thickness. This is thinner than the second level but thicker than the other levels. It is the mental body of a person.

This level stores the thoughts of a person and becomes clearer with the greater clarity in thoughts and vice versa. The thoughts from this body are based on our present experiences and past life experiences, learning and practice of various skills.

The fourth level of Aura is the spiritual body or the soul as it is generally known.

It contains the vital life energy in it. This layer is generally 3 to 4 inches in thickness, but in a spiritually well developed person, the thickness of this layer increases as per spiritual growth level. It was said that Aura of Gautam Buddha was 1 km in thickness. It was actually thickness if this layer.

The fifth level is quite thin. It is about an inch in thickness. It is the past mental body. It contains traces of your past life that you had, before you took birth in this life. This means it has the thoughts and energies that you had stored in your system in your past life.

The sixth level too is thin. It is about an inch too. It's the past emotional body. It has the traces of the emotion of your immediate past life that you had stored in you before this birth.

The seventh level is still thinner. It has the traces of your past physical body. It has the traces of physical issues that were not dissolved and you are carrying from your past lives.

The last 3 layers i.e., the 5th, 6th and 7th layers are the ones that are much thinner and as a result, many people cannot feel it. These last 3 layers are too scanty to see feel or touch.

These are the aura layers of the living, and we see the same number of layers in all living beings, may it be a human being or animal.

This means, even the animals have the same number and order of aura layers.

Only the thing is that the number of stored things in it, reduce in animals as the awareness level reduces.

Anyone who knows to see the aura can check this.

Let us see the aura levels in the living beings in details in an organized manner:

Layer 1:Physical body: the energies absolutely close to physical body are seen to be present here.

Layer 2: Emotional body: Etheric body; brings together all bottom chakras; acupuncture meridians are the energetic lines of this body

Layer 3: Mental body: Inner astral body; around the heart: link between soul and matter; silver cord

Layer 4: Soul: Psychic body; ego; has to be dominated

Layer 5: Past mental body: Spiritual body; brings together all top chakras; each thought draws a line of energy in this body

Layer 6:Past emotional body: Divine body; spiritual potential is linked with the quality and quantity of energy of this body

Layer 7:Past physical body: Outer astral body, in contact with exterior macrocosm

Feeling aura layers needs training. Any one can have this training and know of the aura and its layers and the health conditions of people.

The condition of these aura layers also tell us many things like; where in his aura and what type of energies in which layer of aura; a person has stored from his past life.

Levels of Aura after death

As we have seen above, at death, the aura of a person gets inverted and forms a ball above the head of the person. Then as one is leaving the physical body, its connection with the physical body is cut and it gets detached from the crown chakra of the physical body.

With the connection of this astral body cut from crown chakra, the brain stops working. This is the reason why our medical sciences believe that only when the brain of a person is dead, a person is dead.

The detachment process begins when the aura starts cracking from the feet region. This is the reason why when the feet and knees of any serious person stop giving the jerk reflexes, the doctors tell the relatives to call the nearby relatives as they say there is a little time left for that person.

At death, the astral body is totally formed and detached from physical body. Here the energy body that has left the physical body of a recently dead person and was recently known as the aura; becomes aura of the dead.

This aura has **7 layers** too just as the regular aura. But in this aura, the outermost layer of the original physical body becomes the innermost layer and innermost layer of original physical body becomes the outermost layer.

So in the aura of the dead, the **1**st**outermost layer** is the physical layer of a person that he had in his living **physical body.**

This layer contains all the physical level energies of an individual and is the first one to dissolve after death.

Dissolving this layer takes about 13 to 14 days. So, people keep doing some or the other rituals for the dead during this time.

The **2nd layer** is inside the physical body layer in aura of dead is **emotional body**.

It has all emotions stored that were created during various bodily experiences. This layer is the next to dissolve.

It dissolves after the physical layer of the aura of the dead person has dissolved.

It takes about a year or so to dissolve this layer. But if a person was too much attached, it may take some more time for this layer to dissolve.

The **3rd layer** from outside in aura of dead is the **mental body**.

This contains all thoughts that the dead had stored. More the thoughts, more is the time needed to dissolve this layer.

The **4th layer** of the aura of the dead person, or the astral body, is the soul or spiritual body, just as in regular physical aura.

The **5th layer** is the mental body that was the mental body of the past in the living person. Now it becomes the mental body of the new being that will be born on clearing of aura.

The **6th layer** is the emotional body that was the emotional body of past in the living person. Now it becomes the mental body of the new being that will be born on clearing of aura.

The **7th layer** is the physical body that was the physical body of the past in the living person. Now it becomes the mental body of the new being that will be born on clearing of aura.

These last three layers that become the inner layers of the aura of dead hardly have any baggage, so do not need much clearing.

The aura of the dead keeps floating around in the house where the person was living or around the near and dear of the dead person till the outer three layers are dissolved and the person takes the next birth.

This keeps happening for a number of years. This is the reason why, every year, we perform the death anniversary, of the dead ancestors and let the floating souls know, that we the living heirs of them do remember them.

The main baggage removal from the aura of the dead happens at this level. Out of the three outermost layers; third layer which was mental body of the dead, contains maximum baggage. This aura cleaning process continues till all baggage is dropped off the aura.

After all these three outermost layers of the aura of the dead are dissolved; a soul is ready for next birth.

XII

Dissolving of Astral Body & Problems in dissolving it

Dissolving of Astral Bodies

We saw that astral body is presence of a person after death; and that this is the existence of a person till a person can manifest as next person after next birth.

Let us now see how the astral body gets dissolved and a person is ready for the next birth.

Various thoughts, emotions and experiences are stored in the aura as energy packets and can be read in the form of images.

These are the dense energy packets which are dropped off from the aura of the dead as it is getting cleaned.

This process is just as the process where we discard various unwanted things from house while cleaning it.

Aura of the dead is just as the house of the soul in which it stays till it gets another physical body to be in. naturally, soul keeps shedding all the dense energies from it.

This process happens by default in all souls and as a result, by the time one gets into a new body, the memory of the soul is almost blank.

But we must remember that the stored thoughts and emotions do have their own energy.

Till the time an astral body contains baggage of various thoughts and wishes, the astral body is not dissolved and a person is not ready for next birth.

Sometimes, these wishes are so strong, that the astral body is pulled into some living body causing possession that is commonly known as spirit possession.

Here, the astral body takes over the body of a living person and starts behaving as a living person with that body, by temporarily displacing soul or energy body of that living person's physical body.

This happens when the aura of that person is weak and is thinly connected with physical body. Generally, one's connection with physical body gets weaker with fear or some depression related thoughts.

So, when person with strong attachments and desires, especially, of revenge or so, has died in a family, people nearby, must protect their auras and make connection with their physical body stronger.

When the Astral body is separated from the physical body, for quite some time, soul keeps feeling that he is still alive. So it keeps floating around body and tries to get back in it.

When last rites on the body are performed it realizes that it cannot get back in it and that it is separated from the body for good.

As the physical body gets disintegrated, physical level of Astral body which now is outer most layer of astral body also starts dissolving. This takes about 10 days.

After these 10 days, this outermost layer just remains as a thin cover with nothing much in it. Then the second layer that was mental body, when the person was alive, starts dissolving in the existence.

That means the traces of thoughts and memories that were left in this level of Aura start fading out.

This process for second layer to dissolve completely generally is seen to take about 1 to 3 years. Then this layer just remains as a thin cover in the same way as the first layer.

Then the emotional body of a dead person who is getting ready for next birth, starts dissolving.

Generally, when alive, we are not ready to let go of many emotions.

These stored emotions are stuck to this layer of aura very firmly.

Since this layer contains such emotions and elementals that a person did not easily want to let go, this layer takes rest of the time to dissolve before a person is ready to be born again as another individual.

Generally total period needed for the whole process is somewhat as much as the period for which a person lived. When the dissolving process is over a soul is born again.

This means, if a person has died a normal death at the age of 70, his astral body will take 70 years to dissolve completely and after that the person can take birth again.

It is also observed that those, who commit a suicide, require 100 times the normal time for their emotional body to dissolve.

This means, if a person committed a suicide at the age of 20, he cannot take the next birth for at least 200 years, as the astral body is not ready to leave the baggage and does not want to make the soul ready for next birth.

Problems in dissolving of astral bodies

When process of dissolving the astral bodies starts, some dense energies in astral bodies are seen to cause resistance and then, the process of dissolving slows down.

There are times when such matters get released in space with some life material and start acting like souls.

Many times, we mistake such energy parcels to be ghosts or spirits when they enter any chakra of a person and he starts behaving abnormally due to desire energy in that parcel.

Attachments and strong desires are hard to leave the astral body and so take longer time to dissolve as they contain quite dense energies.

Generally, after death, astral body of a person is still moving around his or her family and keeps staying around the near and dear that were expected to fulfil his desires.

This is the time when the outer layers are dissolving. So, as the desires of the dead about other people around him get fulfilled, the outer layers start getting dissolved.

That is why, we see, a custom to promise the dead about fulfilling his wishes. Here the near and dear promise the soul to fulfil his last wishes so that the soul can release the desire.

Some baggages in the aura of the dead are difficult to dissolve as they are rooted in the life matter in the form of scratches.

Such energies take a longer time to get away and still even after such a long time, at times they are carried further in the next birth.

Such memories are the past life memories that we can remember during our regression sessions and once we remember them, they get detached from the life matter and start getting dissolved.

We are aware of the concept of cleaning a hard-disk in a P.C. before formatting it. We know that even after formatting, the bad sectors still stay back on the hard disk.

The same happens to a soul before he is born again. When the soul is ready to be born again, in the last phase of his stay as an Astral being, be chooses his parents from whom he wants to be born.

Then with the first possible chance, takes its rooting in the womb of his new birth.

As the new physical body to be starts growing, the last traces of the past emotional body that were remaining get wiped out completely.

As a result, when the child is born, it is totally blank and is ready to receive all the experiences a fresh.

Yet here too the scratches on aura stay as past life memories and we can totally wipe them out with scientific past life regression.

XIII

Getting ready to be born again

When all the baggage in various layers in the astral body is dissolved, it becomes light and starts floating at a much higher altitude.

This is the time when the soul is ready for next birth. Then the soul chooses his parents and starts forward into the process of taking birth.

Different souls stay in astral form for different time as we have seen earlier. In normal death, one may take as many years as a person lived for dropping all the baggage.

If a person is totally detached and this means, if a person had reached liberation in his life, he may have no baggage at all, and then he may be ready to choose his next birth as and when he wishes!

But this is seen very rarely and in really advanced spiritual masters.

If a person was too much attached to something, he may take a bit longer time than regular speculated time for dropping baggage.

If a person had committed suicide, he may have a fear of life and as a result, may cling on to its baggage for hundreds of years before he realizes his mistake and drops the baggage to get ready to be born again.

On the other hand, if a person had kind of death where he had to be forcefully out of the body, the desire to be back to life may be very strong. Then a person may not even wait till these bodies are dissolved.

Such a soul may take birth almost immediately that means in a year or two after his death.

This is done as the soul takes over body of new born in the family as it is being formed, or starts his rebirth immediately.

They can be recognised as the old original individuals by the family members as they carry some traces like birth marks or so which the dead had.

Such people may even remember the past life clearly well without any efforts. Also they can say why they are back and what work they want to accomplish.

Also it is believed that some traces of the past memories are there in the new born infants, and so, it is believed that they keep smiling or crying while they are asleep.

We cannot say anything about this with conclusive assurance as there is no way to check these beliefs that people have.

But one thing is certain that a person is not born in any family by accident. He or she has certainly chosen parents before choosing to take birth.

Only we never realise it, so we consider destiny responsible for this.

In case of people who are attached to something, such a choice happens out of obsessive compulsive attraction that pulls him towards the potential parents who have the capacity to fulfil his desires.

In case of liberated souls, there is no such obsessive compulsive attraction, and so such a soul can freely choose his parents.

TRACES OF PAST LIFE MEMORIES IN A PERSON

- Traces of past life memories in person

  - Memory

  - Attitudes

  - Fears & phobias

  - Inner likes & dislikes

  - Fantasies, dreams & drives

XIV
Traces of past life memories

Everyone has past memory traces as we have seen earlier, but the only thing is that we never realise that these are traces of past memories and that with the help of these traces, we can know our past lives!

The basic behaviour traits that differ from person to person are called each person's personality traits.

In spite of the fact that two persons get the same upbringing, they are different!

Even identical twins that share the same DNA pattern, brought up in the same situation are no exception to this!

We take it as just a way in which things are seen in life everywhere! We never try to know why such difference in attitudes and reactions is seen!

But this points out to the presence of past life memories of each person!

These memories are responsible for the attitudes, fears & phobias, one's inner likes and dislikes as well as one's fantasies, drives and dreams!

XV
Memory

Memory is what we remember. Generally, it stands for what we remember out of our experiences in this life, but at times, we feel that we remember things that we have never experienced earlier. These things appear as visions that we cannot understand or explain.

This is why many give the name of imagination to these thoughts. But a simple question appears about these thoughts. Why do we have emotions attached to these thoughts? There is no explanation! These are the memories from our past life!

Our past life memories that had made a very deep impact in our being at that time are still with us! The only thing is that we do not recognise them as our past memories!

Have you seen that some people remember some type of things more easily than others? This is due to their orientation! This orientation comes either from this life or from past life. This means, if there is no orientation to remember a type of things in this life, it is from past life memories!

This holds good both for remembering as well as forgetting. When we have a traumatic memory about something, we try to forget it as fast as possible. Our defence mechanism does this. If we never had any traumatic experience about something and yet we forget that type of instances, we had such experience in past life!

XVI

Attitudes

Many times we have some attitudes that have no explanation. These attitudes are very strong as well at times. These attitudes may include strong attraction or repulsion towards something, place or person.

Resistance to some type of work, strong desire to do some work, irresistible desire to do something and so on. They also may be general tendencies to look at life like chronic hopeful people or chronic pessimists or chronic hypertensive attitude or chronic guilt about any action done and so on!

We cannot do anything about these attitudes! In fact these attitudes hold their roots in past life. If we see past life, we can see why we have these attitudes.

Some people are chronically angry. Also some are always worried. We also see some people who take blame of anything that happens on them. This too is an attitude.

We say that it is the nature of each person and most of the times, the upbringing and the experiences faced by each person are responsible for this, but what about attitudes that have no relevant experience?

Obviously, these attitudes are backed by and created by experiences from past life. On probing into them rightly, we can remember the relevant experience from past life that has given rise to that particular attitude.

XVII

Fears & phobias

Attitudes include unexplained fears and phobias. But since this make a major part of past life memory, they are stated separately.

Fears are learned after having negative experience. Repeated experience of negative event makes a person learn fear about thing that causes this negative experience.

If we touch a hot object, burn our hand badly, we are afraid to touch any hot object in future. Similarly, if we fall in water and start drowning, we fear entering deep water again.

Many times, when a child does not obey parents, they threat him with some imaginary thins and child learns to fear that imagination.

Such fears are learned by humans as well as animals. But if a person is having some experience for the first time in life, there might be fear of unknown and nothing beyond that.

Phobias are inner fears that we are born with. In this life, deep rooted fears that have come from our traumatic experiences too cause phobias. They become part of personality. So phobias are from this birth as well as past life.

Phobia is so strong that one finds it difficult to release the fear generated out of it by way of logical thinking or counselling. It is an irresistible fear that comes as a reflex.

These phobias are mainly of two types, actual and virtual or real and psychological.

Psychology has many phobias listed with their details and explanation. Here is a list of phobias for your reference:

List of phobias:

Here is a complete list of different phobias that people, psychologists and doctors talk about, with their meanings.

General phobias

- **Ablutophobia** – fear of bathing, washing, or cleaning.
- **Acrophobia, Altophobia** – fear of heights.
- **Agoraphobia, Agoraphobia Without History of Panic Disorder** – fear of places or events where escape is impossible or when help is unavailable.
- **Agraphobia** – fear of sexual abuse.
- **Aichmophobia** – fear of sharp or pointed objects (such as a needle or knife).
- **Algophobia** – fear of pain.
- **Agyrophobia** – fear of crossing roads.
- **Androphobia** – fear of men.
- **Anthropophobia** – fear of people or being in a company, a form of **social phobia.**
- **Anthophobia** – fear of flowers.
- **Aquaphobia** – fear of water. Distinct from **Hydrophobia**, a scientific property that makes chemicals averse to interaction with water, as well as an archaic name for rabies.
- **Astraphobia, Astrapophobia, Brontophobia, Keraunophobia** – fear of thunder, lightning and storms; especially common in young children.
- **Atychiphobia**, fear of failure
- **Aviophobia, Aviatophobia** – fear of flying.
- **Bacillophobia, Bacteriophobia, Microbiophobia** – fear of microbes and bacteria.
- **Blood-injection-injury type phobia** – a DSM-IV subtype of specific phobias
- **Chorophobia** - fear of dancing.
- **Cibophobia, Sitophobia** – aversion to food, synonymous to Anorexia nervosa.
- **Claustrophobia** – fear of confined spaces.
- **Coulrophobia** – fear of clowns (not restricted to evil clowns).
- **Decidophobia** – fear of making decisions.

- **Dental phobia, Dentophobia, Odontophobia** – fear of dentists and dental procedures
- **Dysmorphophobia, or body dysmorphic disorder** – a phobic obsession with a real or imaginary body defect.
- **Emetophobia** – fear of vomiting.
- **Ergasiophobia, Ergophobia** – fear of work or functioning, or a surgeon's fear of operating.
- **Ergophobia** – fear of work or functioning.
- **Erotophobia** – fear of sexual love or sexual questions.
- **Erythrophobia** – pathological blushing.
- **Gelotophobia** - fear of being laughed at.
- **Gephyrophobia** – fear of bridges.
- **Genophobia, Coitophobia** – fear of sexual intercourse.
- **Gerascophobia** – fear of growing old or aging.
- **Gerontophobia** – fear of growing old, or a hatred or fear of the elderly.
- **Glossophobia** – fear of speaking in public or of trying to speak.
- **Gymnophobia** – fear of nudity.
- **Gynophobia** – fear of women.
- **Halitophobia** - fear of bad breath.
- **Haptephobia** – fear of being touched.
- **Heliophobia** – fear of sunlight.
- **Hemophobia, Haemophobia** – fear of blood.
- **Hexakosioihexekontahexaphobia** – fear of the number 666.
- **Hoplophobia** – fear of weapons, specifically firearms (Generally a political term but the clinical phobia is also documented).
- **Koumpounophobia** - fear of sewing buttons.
- **Ligyrophobia** – fear of loud noises.
- **Lipophobia** – fear/avoidance of fats in food.
- **Medication phobia** - fear of medications.
- **Megalophobia** - fear of large/oversized objects.
- **Mysophobia** – fear of germs, contamination or dirt.
- **Necrophobia** – fear of death and/or the dead.
- **Neophobia, Cainophobia, Cainotophobia, Cenophobia, Centophobia, Kainolophobia,**– fear of newness, novelty.
- **Nomophobia** – fear of being out of mobile phone contact.
- **Nosophobia** – fear of contracting a disease.
- **Nosocomephobia** - fear of hospitals.
- **Nyctophobia, Achluophobia, Scotophobia** – fear of darkness.

- **Osmophobia, Olfactophobia** – fear of smells.
- **Paraskavedekatriaphobia** – fear of Friday the 13th.
- **Panphobia** – fear of everything or constant fear of an unknown cause.
- **Phasmophobia** - fear of ghosts, spectres or phantasms.
- **Phagophobia** – fear of swallowing.
- **Pharmacophobia** – same as medication phobia.
- **Phobophobia** – fear of having a phobia.
- **Phonophobia** – fear of loud sounds.
- **Pyrophobia** – fear of fire.
- **Radiophobia** – fear of radioactivity or X-rays.
- **Sociophobia** – fear of people or social situations.
- **Scopophobia** – fear of being looked at or stared at.
- **Somniphobia** – fear of sleep.
- **Spectrophobia** – fear of mirrors and one's own reflections.
- **Taphophobia** – fear of grave, or fear of being placed alive in a grave
- **Technophobia** – fear of technology
- **Telephone phobia** -- fear of making or taking phone calls.
- **Tetraphobia** – fear of the number 4.
- **Thanatophobia** – fear of death.
- **Tokophobia** – fear of childbirth.
- **Tomophobia** – fear or anxiety of surgeries/surgical operations
- **Traumatophobia** – fear of having an injury.
- **Triskaidekaphobia, Terdekaphobia** – fear of the number 13.
- **Trypanophobia, Belonephobia,** – fear of needles or injections.
- **Workplace phobia** – fear of the workplace.
- **Xenophobia** – fear of strangers, foreigners, or aliens.

Animal phobias

- **Ailurophobia** – fear/dislike of cats.
- **Animal phobia** - fear of certain animals.
- **Apiphobia,Melissophobia** – fear/dislike of bees
- **Arachnophobia** – fear/dislike of spiders and other arachnids.
- **Chiroptophobia** – fear/dislike of bats.
- **Cynophobia** – fear/dislike of dogs.
- **Entomophobia** – fear/dislike of insects.

- **Equinophobia, Hippophobia** – fear/dislike of horses.
- **Herpetophobia** - fear/dislike of reptiles and/or amphibians.
- **Ichthyophobia** – fear/dislike of fish.
- **Scyphozophobia** – fear/dislike of jellyfish.
- **Musophobia** – fear/dislike of mice and/or rats.
- **Ophidiophobia** – fear/dislike of snakes.
- **Ornithophobia** – fear/dislike of birds.
- **Scoleciphobia** – fear of worms.
- **Zoophobia** – a generic term for animal phobias.

Non-psychological conditions

- **Hydrophobia** – fear of water (a symptom of rabies).
- **Photophobia** – hypersensitivity to light causing aversion to light
- **Phonophobia** – hypersensitivity to sound causing aversion to sounds.
- **Osmophobia** – hypersensitivity to smells causing aversion to odors.

Biology, chemistry

- **Acidophobia, Acidophobic** – preference for non-acidic conditions.
- **Heliophobia, Heliophobic** – aversion to sunlight.
- **Hydrophobia, Hydrophobic** – a property of being repelled by water.
- **Lipophobicity** – a property of fat rejection
- **Ombrophobia** – avoidance of rain
- **Photophobia** -- a tendency to stay out of the light
- **Thermophobia** – aversion to heat.

Prejudices and discrimination

- **Biphobia** – fear/dislike of bisexuals.
- **Christianophobia** - fear/dislike of Christians
- **Ephebiphobia** – fear/dislike of youth.

- **Gerontophobia, Gerascophobia** – fear/dislike of aging or the elderly.
- **Heterophobia** – fear/dislike of heterosexuals.
- **Homophobia** – fear/dislike of homosexuality or homosexuals.
- **Islamophobia** - fear/dislike of Muslims
- **Judeophobia** – fear/dislike of Jews.
- **Lesbophobia** – fear/dislike of lesbian women.
- **Pedophobia, Pediophobia** – fear/dislike of children.
- **Psychophobia** – fear/dislike of mental illness or the mentally ill.
- **Transphobia** – fear/dislike of transgender or transsexual people.
- **Xenophobia** – fear/dislike of foreigners.

These phobias are seen commonly in many people and many are just used to them, so do not feel that there is anything different in them, actually, they are gateways to past. We all are aware of phobias that we and our dear ones have, but we don't realise that these are the memories that can take us into our past life and help us to release that extra baggage which we were carrying for births and is also causing obstacles in our present life.

As child, I had phobia against lightening. But reason was, when I was about 10 months, lightening had crashed on electric pole just next to me; and adjacent building had caught fire due to that. That memory had created this phobia and awareness of it made it disappear!

But what about fear of being eaten by a tiger when you have never seen a tiger in your whole life? Same goes true of fear of being bitten by a snake while putting feet in water even if this water happens to be from seashore where there is no snake heard of! Also if this person having this fear has never seen a snake in his life, we have only one conclusion left and that is, this fear has come from his past life!

XVIII
Inner Likes & Dislikes

People differ in choices in spite of getting same upbringing. So, likes, dislikes, comforts, and fears that they have too differ.

We say that these choices depend on their inner nature, but then also we must have to remember that a person develops any like or dislike because of favourable or unfavourable experience.

If this experience has happened in this life, we know about it, and if not, then it has happened in our past life.

It is strongly believed that all our likes and dislikes that we have are generated in us purely depend on our experiences and their repetitions.

An experience that has given us repeated favourable result is desired and so is liked, whereas any experience that has produced repeated unfavourable result is not desired and so is disliked.

This is the cause of the likes and dislikes we develop in life. But as far as we know, this holds good of experienced and known things. But likes and dislikes do not follow this rule every time.

We do have likes and dislikes and even cravings about the things and the experiences that we have never had in our life.

There cannot be any reasonable explanation about them. At the most one may say that these are the feelings based on imagination caused due to similarity in something that one knows.

Just notice around as well as within your own self and you will realise.

These likes and dislikes can be about anything like the type of place, person, animal, plant, clothes, event, noise, music, activity, mode of transport, way of living, attitude towards attitudes shown by some people, or any such thing.

If a person is in a situation for the first time in his life, and if he is showing some strong reaction of like or dislike of this type, such an expression is certainly not reasonable.

When there is space for imagination due to similar experience or due to fears generated due to storied heard about something in the past, one may say that these likes and dislikes are due to these stories.

But in cases, where imagination factor too is absent, we can certainly conclude that the reaction has some roots in the past.

The likes and dislikes of the past are due to experiences we had in the past life and may be due to some trauma, they get carried forward in this life.

So we experience them without any reasonable ground in this life. We can recognize these likes and dislikes as coming from the past when we know that there is no base of experience behind them.

But for defining this we must thoroughly check the grounds of our likes and dislikes. Once we are sure that they have no roots in this life, we can use them as gate ways to past life.

XIX

Dreams, Desires, Drives & Fantasies

We have some dreams, desires, wishes and fantasies. They depend on our upbringing.

We learn to have some desires and wishes as per the things we learn in life from people around us.

Whatever we have, we learn to wish just a little bit more than that!

A child of a government servant may dream of having a job in corporate sector, but may not dream of owning a corporate office with a million employees.

This example will show the general limitations of the dreams fantasies and desires of people.

But there are times when the dreams cross these limits.

A child of a millionaire may behave as well as think like a popper and vice versa.

Sometimes, we find that a person starts saying right from childhood that he wants to take up some profession, and this choice does not change with age as in other children.

Dreams of some people do come true. Then they are called visions.

The persons, who makes them come true, are called visionary.

But no one knows how one has a vision. No one knows how a visionary is mostly born. No one can say why and how a visionary is born in any family. No one can say why people have dreams about owning or making things they cannot even imagine to experience. No one knows why some people have fantasies that others around them never understand.

Then people say that such dreams, of so called impossible things, are madness. But one has to realize that these dreams have some inner drive that generated them.

They do pose questions that need to be probed into.

Some people have strong inner drives to do something either good or bad.

We do find that in a hard core non-vegetarian family, someone is born who does not even choose to look at any non-vegetarian food right from his early childhood. Also it may happen other way.

At times, in a family that is very sober and soft spoken, a person is born who from his infancy and toddler hood, is seen to be too aggressive, abusive and noisy.

Such things make us feel that there is something wrong. But we do not know what is wrong here. The different traits these people show have certainly not come from their family upbringing.

But we fail to trace the roots of these traits.

People have different dreams, different desires, create different stories on seeing the same thing, fantasise in different ways, have different inner drives, and all these traits are called individual differences.

Psychology says that no two individuals are the same. Even identical twins, who share the same heredity, same sets of genes and chromosomes, differ in many ways.

They differ in their likes, dislikes, dreams and visions in spite of same upbringing that they get. Study of such events lead us to only one answer and that is past life.

CONCEPTS AND THINGS RELATED TO PAST LIFE

- Problems arising due to past life
- Concept of karma
- Obsessive compulsive rebirth
- Freedom from obsessive compulsive rebirth
- Liberation=freedom from obsessive compulsion
- Repeatedly facing forced situations
- Repeated event patterns that depress
- Ailments without visible cause
- Obsessive compulsive relationships
- Problems that take away all energy
- Likes or dislikes without reason

XX

Problems arising due to past life

We are certainly not interested in knowing about past life just for fun sake! We want to know about it, so that we can make use of what we remember, in our present life, in order to improve it.

Everyone wants to bring harmony in the life. If remembering past life can help us to handle present life problems, then we must do it. We can solve present problems by handling their roots in past life.

But for saying that present problem has roots in past, and we must know this conclusively before saying so. If not, we may just end up in hiding behind the excuse of past life in order to escape the responsibility of mistakes and irresponsible behaviour on our part.

We can do scientific introspection in order to know this. While doing this, we must be aware of excuses our subconscious mind gives us and tries to show that we are not guilty of the problem we have faced. Every time, when we face a problem, we must first accept its responsibility and then start looking for its cause.

When we do not know why we face a situation or have obsessive compulsive reactions that repeatedly put us in a mess, we need to look into our past for answers.

XXI
Concept of karma

People have different notions of a simple thing called karma.

They say that if we have done wrong things in past life, we suffer the punishment of it in the present life.

So, generally, people who have this notion, hardly have sympathy for the suffering people.

They just say that people suffer due to their own past lie karmas. This is an attitude that makes a person escape his responsibility towards those who need our help.

We need to make them realise that they are actually running a pattern of suffering due to their past life attitudes and that they need help to come out of this trap.

But instead of doing so, people say that may be they have harmed a person who is harming them, in past life; so, they should keep taking the harm.

I have seen Karmas in auras of people.

I have known that karmas are knots of conflict in the aura of a person.

When we do something and then repent or want to do something, but do not want it at the same time, the energies sent by us in both directions at the same time, conflict and form a knot of energy in aura.

These knots obstruct the energies that go in that particular direction, and one fails to achieve the goal.

Then whenever we try to do that kind of act or interact with a person about whom such a knot is formed, we get stuck with conversation that has formed the knot.

This may happen in this life or in one of the past lives.

We remember conversations & conflicts of this life, but not past.

So when we try to introspect honestly, we come across inner conversations form this life, but cannot get into the inner conversations of past clearly.

We just have some strong pull that we cannot explain.

Then, we get confused. We say that it is some fear or confusion that is pulling, but that cannot be understood.

People call them past life karmas. People also say that we have these karmas because of our mistakes in past life.

But actually, this is just escapist myth. When one does not want to help any person either because one doesn't know how to help or because the trouble of that person has a potential to help or benefit him, one ends up saying above things as a past life explanation.

Of course, when we keep hearing this from a large number of people, we also start taking this to be true. This is how actually, the myth about past life sins has originated.

We are also encouraged to repent and say sorry for things that we do not feel are wrong, but others call wrong. Such repentance may also cause knots of karmas. When these knots grow stronger, they are carried in future.

Whatever we find as knots of karmas from past lives, are such knots that the aura had developed or were carried from still previous past, in that past life. There are knots that might be created hundreds of years back.

XXII

Obsessive compulsive rebirth

At times these knots pull us back to life and make us take birth in a certain family or near some people. This is obsessive compulsive re-birth.

We feel some pulls of attractions or repulsions that we never understand but still experience strongly. These are the results of the obsessive compulsive part of our unfulfilled desires in past life.

These desires make us take birth in a certain place or in a certain manner and make us develop certain relations. Those who interpret this religiously call this as Karma, but then interpretations given of Karma differ from place to place and religion to religion. There is no universal interpretation.

We can give a universal interpretation to this thing called Karma to call it as obsessive compulsive re-birth. This means, if one had some desires that were not fulfilled and if these desires were really strong, the soul refuses to discard them in cleansing process. Then it takes birth to fulfil these desires.

Now in the new birth, the soul moves towards fulfilling those desires, but still the innate tendencies stay and one keeps getting same obstacles that one had faced in past life. This is the reason why we need to get free from this obsessive compulsiveness behind birth as well as behind our behaviour.

But at times the obstacles are so strong that we feel stuck. At such times past life healing helps.

XXIII

Freedom from obsessive compulsive rebirth

As we learn to see the past life, we also learn how to get free from this obsessive compulsive pull of desires, likes and dislikes.

Then we can detach from desires that were in past life, but have no value in present one.

As we learn to see past life, we can start knowing various pulls we have been feeling in our life.

Some of these pulls have roots here in this life and we can work on them consciously, but we cannot detect the roots of some pulls. Then we need to look into our past for these roots.

As we do this, we can see what was the thing in past that had created the desire to achieve or avoid a particular thing, experience, person or event.

This knowledge is enough to discard it, as then we know that in this life the pull has no value.

Just as at times things are stored in our home.

We have never seen or used them, but they are still there.

They keep creating clutter. But the moment we check them and find them useless for present, we discard them.

Same is the case with these pulls. The moment they are detected and found useless they are out.

So, to overcome obsessive compulsive rebirth, we must keep in mind that we must not store any strong desires that may have power to be carried to next life, and detect and discard all past pulls of such desires.

XXIV

Liberation = freedom from obsessive compulsion

Technically speaking, this discarding of pulls itself is real liberation.

People define liberation in many ways. Some people say it is freedom from the cycle of life and death, some say it is merging with God.

But why we must achieve liberation is something no one has stated categorically, and may be this is the reason why only those who are so called inclined towards spirituality talk of things like liberation and for others it is an unreachable dream.

In fact if we understand the obsessive compulsive nature of our re-birth desires and pulls, we can understand what attachment is.

Attachment is getting entangled to something without any visible reason. Also attachment is keeping this entanglement beyond reasonable limit.

Even if we are attached for any practical purpose, we must know till where to take it and where to discard it.

We know which thing is useful or useless in home or office, but most of the times, we do not know which thought is useful or useless in our mind.

This knowledge is the basis of real knowledge of inner self. It helps us discard all obsessive compulsions and then we can experience real liberation.

After achieving such liberation, a soul is not pulled into obsessive compulsive re-birth.

Then one can choose to take the next birth as, where and when one wants.

Liberation is not freedom from life or death.

It is freedom from obsessive compulsions in life and death.

The moment we understand this real meaning of liberation we understand that this IS the real goal of every person in his life.

One wants to live life full of happiness and freedom.

Since we do not understand meaning of words like liberation, we accept meaning given to them by people without actual knowledge.

Then we take those words to be true and trust them.

Then if such meaning appears to be beyond our reach, we say it is something that only highly spiritual people can achieve.

But actually this is not so. If this planet is created to have life on it, what is the sense of eliminating the possibility of our future life?

It is said that liberation is being one with God.

But if we accept that God is the building material of the universe, and soul is object in universe, then we can know that merging the soul with the original building material means destroying and recycling the soul.

We destroy & recycle only useless things from our home or vicinity. We retain all useful things.

If this rule applies to us, then it applies to the universal consciousness too.

If a soul is useful to the world, universal consciousness will never destroy or recycle it.

So, if a person is good, pious and religious, and if he becomes still better, his soul will never be recycled.

But still people keep becoming better and more useful to humanity and then keep wishing that their soul must be recycled. To get recycled, soul must be really bad, dangerous or worthless.

If a soul is not useful in universe, universal consciousness will recycle it.

This means, if we have to accept the interpretation of liberation that is given by majority of scholars, we must know that the demons killed by Gods got liberation as their souls needed to be recycled.

This is stated in many religious stories too. But if a useless soul is recycled, naturally a useful is not.

So liberation does not mean recycling of the soul.

So the natural outcome of this is that liberation is freedom from attachments, but we cannot live in society without attachments, so total freedom from attachments is impossible.

But freedom from attachments that lead to obsessive compulsions must be discarded.

This is also main aim of past life healing.

This means, when we learn past life healing and keep practicing it regularly to heal various issues in our present life, we can get released from the stored obsessive compulsions and eventually reach most desired but apparently unreachable stage called liberation.

From above discussion, it is clear that liberation is not merging with GOD and having our soul destroyed.

It is retaining our identity, but removing all tags of attachment stuck to soul. Since real liberation is this, all can get it.

XXV

Repeatedly Facing some situations

We face some situations repeatedly in spite of strong efforts to avoid them. We feel helpless at times and at times we feel that some people are playing some tricks on us.

But if we look in greater details, we can see that these are due to past life knots that are also commonly known as karmas. We do things to release them but in vain.

So we must know that these can get released only when we get aware of those knots by seeing past life.

When we face situations we wish to come out, but unknowingly behave in a particular way and get deeper into a problem, everyone around us finds our behaviour abnormal.

We never realise what happens to us when we face these situations and why we behave in such obsessive compulsive manner. People end up saying that some one has done black magic.

But in fact we give this reaction for that type of situation from our past life experiences. If we probe into subconscious mind about these reactions, we will find some deep rooted fears or negative emotions that trigger these reactions in us about that type of situations.

We cannot help the reactions at this time as these reactions are very strong and quick and as a result; we can't help reacting in that way.

After reacting, we realise that we must not have reacted that way, but by then, we find that the time is gone and damage is done.

In fact deep rooted thoughts, emotions or fears make us face some situations forcibly due to their negative attachment to them.

For example, sometimes, some people get very angry on seeing a child being scolded or beaten.

The reaction of these people is hyper. But that person cannot control the reaction.

On seeing the childhood of a person, anyone can say that he or she had a perfectly happy childhood, but still this attitude is there.

On asking about this attitude, the person may say, "I don't know why I reacted like that, but I cannot control myself when I see some one scolding or beating a child!"

People need support to handle such reactions that repeatedly put them in soup.

But very few realise the need of help. Also, those who feel the need of support keep wasting their time, energy & money visiting counsellors and similar individuals.

Some waste money on quacks who claim to remove the so called black magic.

Some waste on astrologers to perform rituals. But when nothing helps, people give thought about past life regression and healing.

If this last choice becomes first, lot of effective time, energy & money can be saved.

If we see our past life under the presence of a qualified healer who can take you in your past life without hypnotising you, you can know what went wrong at what time, and then the knots will start dissolving.

Then we can consciously handle these reactions.

XXVI
Repeated depressing event patterns

It is understood to be depressed due to some valid reason, but getting depressed for no reason is something that needs attention. Some event patterns depress without reason

We generally take this baseless depression as an attempt made by a person to escape responsibilities.

In a way this is right. When one does not want to take responsibility, one says that one is depressed or sick. This helps a person get sympathy and also escape responsibility.

Also there are some situations in life that depress some and strengthen others.

This means, on facing a situation, one person may get depressed, while, other may feel stronger in the same situation.

It is difficult to believe that same experience can make some one positive and some other persons negative.

This proves that the situation in itself is neither depressing nor strengthening.

So, we have to admit that the reaction pattern has connection with past life memories.

It is past life memory about it that one has stored that causes this.

These patterns are caused by individual events or situations or places or site of some type of persons or so.

The main thing about these patterns is that they never trigger normal reaction in the persons having them.

The persons having such patterns have some peculiar reaction to them.

As an example of this we may check a simple reaction after seeing a cat or a dog. Some people may be friendly or normal while some may scream out of fear.

In fact this scream also scares the poor animal. This is certainly not a normal reaction.

On the top of that, some of these people feel depressed at the site of such animals or some birds or things like that.

They feel that now, something bad is going to happen.

Some people feel depressed while seeing fights even from movies while some tremble out of fear on seeing snake even on screen.

The worst experience is getting into trap of failures.

When a person repeatedly keeps failing in job or relationship or business, he feels depressed, frustrated, lost, but does not know how to come out the vicious circle of the failure trap.

Many times, one finds that one invites situations to fail.

But even after one realizes that one is inviting failures, one cannot help it and cannot stop sending such invites.

The failure traps & obsessive compulsive attracting of situations to fail is clear indication that one has brought that pattern from past & needs to be probed in by scientific regression.

XXVII

Ailments without visible cause

We also find people falling sick for no reason at times. Medical tests are normal and yet they show symptoms of some ailments. At times, even medicines do not work.

They only produce side effects & develop complications.

Then people think of all possible unreasonable reasons like spirit possession, black magic etc. & start running after remedies for such things. But these ways also don't work.

Then people get depressed & confused.

This all happens because such ailments have their roots in the past life of that person and once the past life is healed, the sickness is healed.

Many times, such past life based ailments are of curious types.

They may not be actually related to any known ailment at all.

It may be something like pain in some body part after getting hit by a bullet that may trigger out of nowhere at a certain age when in previous life, person had died when bullet hit him.

It may be sudden pain in heart as if some thing is piercing heart, when all tests are perfect and person is showing no variations in E.C.G. after stress test as well.

We cannot give any logical or medical explanation to these problems.

Yet the problem persists. All medical tests give normal reports.

Then naturally one fails to understand why the problem is there.

At such times one may think of various kinds of explanations like black magic.

It might be past life memory of some wound or shock, when life had ended.

Such memories emerge approximately at the same time in this age, when in past life, the life of a person had ended, as at that time, the memory starts surfacing.

Then one gets restless due to the fear and anticipation of death.

Some people visualize some fearful things regularly as dreams or hallucinations.

Some people have some unimaginable irrelevant fears repeatedly arising in their mind for no reason.

In such situations in spite of having medically perfect health, some people keep getting visions that someone is coming to kill them, or someone is shooting them or someone is throwing them from a cliff or someone is hitting them or they are accidently or forcibly consuming some poison or they are falling down from cliff or such height or meeting with an accident of a particular type or so on.

These visions differ from person to person, but they are irresistible and very strong and accompany ailment symptoms that are medically absent.

This type of ailments, have no known or visible cause and are healed only and only on healing past life issue connected with them.

So instead of wasting time, money and energy on repeatedly doing things that do not work if one helps the patient to see his past life and cause of the trauma and let him realize that now the trauma causing situation is not there; so he need not carry the fears due to that situation.

Then one may see miraculous improvement in the state of the patient.

Once the past memory related to the ailment is spotted, remembered and released, ailment too vanishes with the memory and person starts enjoying great health again.

XXVIII

Obsessive compulsive relationships

Some people have obsessive compulsive relationships with certain people or personality types. These relations cannot be explained or understood by known logic. People who have such relations are called crazy. These relations are due to attractions or repulsions from past.

If we were friendly with someone in past life, we tend to be friendly with that person again in this life whenever we meet him. But at such times, neither of the two realise why they are so much comfortable with each other in their very first meeting.

In fact even if they have met for the first time in this life, it is just a continuation of their relation from past. So there is no gap and they feel as if they know each other for ages! Same is the case with past aversions and repulsions. If someone has hurt us in the past life, then in this life too, as soon as we see that person, we feel aversion towards that person and we try to keep away from that person.

May be at that time, the person we are keeping away from may never realise why we are reacting like this to him or her. The relation develops some tension for no reason if that person is closely related to us. So, when one feels such negative feeling for no reason for any close person, one has to check the past life factor related to it. This is how we can track the presence of past life from relations.

XXIX

Problems that take away all energy

Some problems or situations take away all energy of a person to drain him completely. This may not happen to everyone, but for some people, some typical problems drain all energy. That person is taken as panic. But it is not so.

This happens due to the past life impact when the life of that person had ended trying to handle that type of situation. As a result, when one faces the same type of situation in this life, he starts reacting in the same way as he had reacted in the past.

He starts losing all his energy as in past life, he had lost his strength and his life had ended without coming out of the situation or without succeeding to solve the problem. So, he tries his level best to come out of that situation in this life, but has a fear that even in this life, he will not succeed.

This drains him totally and he feels weak and depressed while fighting that situation or problem. Then he develops pessimistic attitude and keeps repeating the same mistake that he had done in past life.

So, at such times, he needs support to to look at the situation with a different angle so that he can handle it better without getting drained.

Seeing past life and seeing mistakes of past life in such situations helps.

Once a person finds out past life issues connected with that problem, he can handle that problem successfully.

Then that type of situations never drain his energies!

XXX
Likes or dislikes without reason

Every person has some likes and dislikes that have no logical reason or experiences in this life time.

But, still people have strong likes or dislikes about some things that they see or experience for the first time in life.

We believe that a person likes a thing or act that has given him repeated pleasant experience.

This means, either by doing a particular action or approaching a particular thing, a person gets pleasure, or a thing that gives him pleasure appears in front of him.

Similarly, person dislikes a thing or action that has given him repeated unpleasant experience.

This means, either by doing a particular act or approaching a particular thing, a person gets pain, or a thing that gives him pain appears in front of him.

The memories of experiences are stored in our brain.

They determine connections of various experiences as pleasant or unpleasant.

Our memories determine our likes and dislikes in the long run.

Whenever we like or dislike anything, if we try to look back in our memory, we can point out to these things that cause these likes and dislikes.

Some likes as well as dislikes can be traced back in our childhood.

At times, some things had given great pleasure to us as a child, so, we are happy to see or experience those things. Same holds good for reverse too.

If we were greatly hurt as a child due to some thing, experience, or person, then even after growing up, we dislike and repel that thing, experience or person type.

Anyone can check the truth of this by looking into the likes and dislikes in one's own life.

On introspection, one is sure to know that this is true and that every like and dislike has to have a solid foundation of our own positive or negative past experience.

But there are instances when we cannot find out memories about our likes and dislikes and yet our likes and dislikes are very strong.

We like or dislike some things or events or persons, but never know why.

Our mind gets tired if we try to look back for its trace in our childhood.

If we try to strain our memory, we even develop headache or experience breathlessness while searching root cause of strong dislike without known ground.

The analysis of like-dislike pattern seen above shows very clearly that likes and dislikes must have memory of supporting events.

But if we cannot find memories of such pleasure or pain are not in this life memory inventory; it only means that the memories leading to these likes or dislikes are carried in our system from our past life.

We can treat these unexplained liked and dislikes as the gateways that can take a person into his past life memories.

HEALING PAST LIFE TRAUMAS

- Healing past life traumas

- Past life traumas

- Knowing the traces

- Getting help of master

- Remembering & healing trauma

XXXI
Healing past life traumas

To know our past life is a subject of curiosity.

But remember; as we start seeing our past life, in beginning, we can easily remember only the events that have had caused severe trauma or death.

Such memories are easily accessible when we start probing into our past; as these are memories with deep impact on soul.

We always urge that the first attempt of seeing past life has to be under able supervision of a sufficiently experienced master who has had enough practice of taking people into past life.

This is because, if going into past life is tried on one's own or in presence of one who is doing it unprofessionally, it may cause grave problems on physical or mental plane.

This is because when one is seeing past life for the first time, one is crossing a death barrier.

When one is doing this, one actually expeiences death and knows that it was just a memory.

But while doing it, one needs the presence of super-powerful positive energy around a person that can help this transition easier.

So do remember that helping oneself as well as others is good, and so is helping someone get into past life to handle past life traumas.

But know that this has to be done professionally. One may put patient in a greater soup by unprofessional approach.

When a professional master takes you in past life; he knows how to handle transition of memory during death barrier cross. Absence of care here, may give rise to any problem.

So avoid risk.

Let master help through in first time death barrier for by past life healing without hypnosis, then you can get a multiple entry visa into your past lives and keep seeing your past by yourself as and when you choose.

We have seen how to detect events that can work as gate ways to past life.

Now we have to see how to heal these traumas and make our present life better.

Of course, for healing these events, we must remember them by remembering the past and this must be done under a masters' guidance if you are doing it for the first time.

The proper past life healing training sessions are held by me as well by masters trained by me.

This training can also be received by emails by people who do not have a master nearby.

XXXII

Past life traumas

Any event that leaves a very deep impact of shock on our mind is Trauma.

It shakes and shatters our being and one needs a lot of time and healing to overcome it.

A trauma may be caused due to physical or psychological injury.

If a person stays alive after experiencing a trauma, he can recover and get over it.

Then after some days or years, he may even forget about that trauma.

But if a person dies during the experience of it, it stays as an impression on the soul and is carried as a past life trauma in the next birth and further births that follow.

Past life traumas are traumas that have caused the end of our past life.

Then similar event types cause partial remembrance of past life traumas in our present life.

Generally it is seen that a person gets a shock on having experience similar to past life traumas.

Even the thought or sight of that type of event is strongly disliked by a person.

This can be noticed by the strong reactions of people on meeting with events or people in real life, stories or even movies.

Some people cannot stand the sight of a snake or a lion or tiger even on the screen while watching a movie.

Some cannot stand violence on screen or do not even like to hear any news about violence and war or riots. These people show reasonably strong aversion to the said events or sights.

We may say that the person is getting unnecessarily hyper and then we also try to explain the person that he must not react in that way, but he says that he cannot help the reaction.

He also says that he knows that it is not fair to react like that, but he has no control over his reaction.

He then even apologises for his reactions if he has offended others during that reactive phase of behaviour.

Such reactions indicate past life traumas when they are very strong and unnatural.

These traumas are the events that have caused our death in one of our many past lives and as a result, we have learned to have a strong negative reaction towards the events that have a potential to produce them or their memories.

Remembering such traumas is painful, but retaining their scars is painful for longer time, so it is a better idea to remember them and remove the scars for good.

To do this individually without support is difficult and painful, but the past life healing master helps us do this effectively with relatively lesser pain.

While knowing about our past lives, we do search through the traumas and work to detect and heal them with their root cause. This can make our future life better.

This means memories of past life traumas that we are carrying from many past lives can be detected, healed and released so that our present life is free from their effects. Almost everyone has the trauma memories, so all can see past life.

XXXIII

Knowing the traces

As we saw above, past life traumas are carried as unexplained phobias, strong dislikes or any such feelings. Their roots cannot be traced in any experiences of a person's present life. But they make a person react strongly.

Generally, fears are learned by negative experiences that one has and due to these experiences, one learns to fear. He also learns to avoid things and events that may make a person have that experience again.

But in case of phobias, one has no such experiences from the known life. So, we have to conclude that one has carried these fears from his past life experiences and traumas.

About such phenomenon when we think scientifically, we can say that as various layers of Aura are getting cleaned up, some hard and sticky substance that has been created out of some traumas and shocks still remains in the life material or aura of an individual.

Just as the bad patches remain in the hard disk even after we have cleaned it completely in order to format again; these sticky substances still remain after clean up of memories from aura.

These substances carry the traces of your past life memories.

Each memory stored in the life material is in coded form and after decoding by the brain, it appears in the form of images. So our memories are stored as images and not words.

The images stored are remembered by us at certain times and when they have power of causing fear, one is afraid of event or sight that resembles these images.

When such images come along with birth, they are said to be from past life. So, they are past life traces.

Generally phobias in people are results of these past life memory traces carried by these sticky substances.

Even if we try to remember the image, we may get some hazy image about the cause but it may not be very clear.

To make it clear, we need to learn how to focus effectively on such memories and for that we must also learn to cross the death barrio that prevents clear vision of that memory.

Also, most of the phobias that we are clearly aware of are not from our immediate past birth, but are from births prior to that.

We have seen that with every birth, the aura state keeps reversing, so, the physical, mental, emotional layers of one life, become the past life in the next, and again become present in the life after that.

So at times, when our phobia belongs to life prior to immediate past, the traces may also be in the layer that is right now our present physical, mental or emotional level.

When a past life memory is found in our present aura, we must know that it was not in the last birth but in the birth before that.

May be this is the reason why when we see past life for the first time, mostly one remembers events at least about 100 years back or so.

XXXIV

Getting help of a master

When one is trying to detect these traces and analyse them, there are times when one feels very restless. One does not even want to think of these things or events one is working to remember. Then, one just starts thinking or discussing something else on other subject.

These are the times when one wants to even drop the idea of detecting traces of past life trauma and probing into them for detecting and healing memory related to it. One feels that it is just a waste of time and energy and nothing like this is going to happen. One also says then that there is nothing like past life.

All these are the symptoms that one is hitting right memory chord from our memory directory. But since that memory is depressing, it makes one restless. The depressing emotion that overflows from that suppressed memory makes us try to escape the memory and push it back in the subconscious mind by thinking of something else or doing something else.

Of course, this is not only true for past life memories; the same rule applies even to our regular memories where we tend to ignore some things or work even if we know that it is important. Normally we never realise why we often change some subjects or avoid some types of work, but now while seeing the past life, we are discussing the roots of this simple phenomenon seen in everyday life.

This type of avoidance is shown by us about any memory or work because that memory or task had given us pain sometime in the past and there is a bitter memory of that task or event which prevents us from following up that task or remembering that event.

When this happens about remembering past life memory, at times, it is not just the mind but also the body that participates in the game of pushing the memory we are trying to remember, back in our subconscious mind.

Then we start feeling breathless or get some severe pain somewhere in the body. At times, the pain is so severe that we have to leave everything else and attend to the pain.

This is the time when a master's help is needed. The master teacher who helps you see the past life heals pains and works on resistance shown by seeker's mind and body to this past memory.

A master helps a person to detect past life traumas by asking right questions. He also explains the need to detect these traumas and benefit of remembering and healing them. He explains how we can improve our present once these past memories are detected and healed.

But of course trying this without master is certainly inviting problems as then seeker may not know how to handle the resistance then may be the pain that surfaces with efforts of remembering past, may continue and even medication may not help here.

XXXV

Remembering & Healing Trauma

When master intervenes the resistance and helps a person to probe into the traumatic memories, one can easily remember them and then as these memories of past life traumas surface, they get healed as they start losing their power to cause problems in our present.

One can heal every memory of past life trauma and its memory in this manner. Once this is done, the past life memory gets cleared and then that trauma loses its power to create pains as well as problems in our present life.

We have seen above that the knots in the aura or energy body are the actual causes of obstacles in our life. When the energies sent by us stop at the knots, we stumble in life and then cannot move further in that direction.

So we know very well that these stumbling blocks must be removed from our life. But most of us do not know how to do it.

Remembering the past life trauma and letting one's soul realise that the event which caused pain had happened in the past life and so, one need not worry about that event in this life is enough to heal the traumas.

Once traumas from past life are healed, many issues that keep blocking the progress and good health of a person get dissolved and one starts getting all the success one was always longing for.

GETTING HELP FROM PAST LIFE MEMORIES

- Getting help from past life memories

- Hidden treasures in past life memories

- Getting help of healer to find hidden treasures

- Using this hidden treasure in present life

- Developing talents brought from past

XXXVI

Getting help from past life memories

Once we cross the death-barrier, we can see and check other traces of our past life too. These traces are in the forms of likes that have no explanation or cravings about doing some tasks. When we try to get into these memories by unlocking these good past life memories, may lead us to memories about our skills and powers that we had in various past lives.

If we can have an access to this, we may find a great treasure with the help of which we may be able to use our past life skills. This can help us progress in life by having some additional help of skills that we had learned, and mastered in past lives.

Just as we get rid of past life traumas to make life better; we can also enrich our life by receiving help from memories about past skills; thereby learning these skills almost again.

Just as we release memories of past life traumas, we refresh and revive the memories of skills and powers of past life, so that they become available to us once again.

The process followed for this is the same as the process followed for searching for traumas. The only difference is that here there is not much pain and since we are seeing these good memories after crossing death barrier, we can remember them more easily.

This means, good memory treasures of past are available only after we have seen the first past life in presence of master, and then cleared some past life traumas by ourselves.

XXXVII

Hidden treasures in past life memories

As we have seen just now; our past life memories have some treasures hidden in them. These are some special abilities and skills we had in our past life. We were using them in our past life and may be were known to be masters of those abilities or skills. In this life, it is not necessary that we are pursuing the same.

But unlocking of the past life memories can help us access these skills again. Then we can use them in our present life to improve our present skills or even take up the work that gets unlocked in this process with memory of our past life skills. This may start a new great chapter in our life. But it is not possible to tap these memories to get maximum benefit out of them unless we see our past life clearly.

In the presence of a master one can see our first past life and then one can see past lives as and when one wants. Initially, we must clear as much traumas and problems as we can. Once we feel that we are done with traumas and that now nothing blocks our path towards success, we may move towards our search of past treasures. Then we can tap our past life treasures of skills as well as different abilities and use them in this life.

These hidden treasures that come from past life are surfaced as some unreasonable likes and drive to do some things.

In some people the past life treasures are evident right from birth. These are people born with some special abilities and talents like good ear for music or good mathematical skills etc. these abilities and skills indicate the treasures that can be fully used after tapping them and opening up the relevant memory.

These are not trauma related memories, so, one cannot tap them in the beginning of our journey of seeing past life. As we have seen above, the first memory that one must see while starting to see past life has to be a trauma related one as it takes us through the death barrier. Then one can tap and detect these treasures and use them.

It is interesting to access such treasures from our past as these treasures are the abilities of master skills that we were used to make our life better in past. May be the living conditions of past needed us to use them in a particular manner, but now in the present life style, we may use them in a way that helps us improve our present life.

These hidden treasures are like some extra bonus our past gives us as we unload the baggage of past and make our souls lighter. Naturally, we can treat it as a gift.

But such good memories too have a dark lining as these skills too stayed in our system just because the uninstall file was missing in our system for them. This can happen only when one had died while using those skills.

XXXVIII

Getting help of healer to find hidden treasures

For searching the hidden treasures, one can work on oneself if one is trained, and take help of healer if not trained. At times, after getting trained to see past life and seeing the first past with the help of healer, one still feels that resistance towards some inner issue is too much. At times, this inner resistance comes in the way of actual memory. Then we deviate from actual memory & start creating things and stories that only lead to imagination. At such one may still seek help of master or have recap session of past life healing with master healer.

One may also need to have recap session with the master for treasure hunt from past. The healer can help us see hidden treasures from past life by asking different questions. These questions relate to present memory or involve some free imagination of stories that actually lead to past life memory about some excellence or special ability.

Once one has gone into one's past with the help of master, with received training, one can also ask these questions to one's own self and see one's past treasures or may form a group of past life healers who have already crossed death barrier & help each other in this.

Such a group of past life practitioners can be of great help to each other in searching various memories & treasures hidden in past.

Such support group can also be useful when we find ourselves running away from some issue we want to handle and need help.

Yet, it is necessary to remember very well that seeking help from just such support group instead of crossing death barrier in the presence of a master, is not advisable.

Also, any person who has learned past life healing but not become a master in past life healing by taking proper teacher's training, must not try to probe into past of person who has not crossed death barrier. It is dangerous.

To find the hidden treasures, one may look into our interests and aptitudes. Then check the root of these interests and aptitudes. If we find that the root of these interests is nowhere in the present life experiences, we can say that they have come from past lives.

Same rule applies for aptitudes as well. If some skill is seen in any family and one is watching it regularly since childhood, one can understand having the aptitude. But when one has never seen any skill used by any other person in family or friends or neighbourhood or anywhere what so ever, then, if we find that a person shows aptitude of that skill, we have to trace the roots of that aptitude in past.

The treasure search goes just as we do for trauma search and here too we can go on creating story on the basis of that particular interest or aptitude we want to find; without any limits of time, place or any other thing.

XXXIX

Using this hidden treasure in present life

When one finds out the hidden treasures, in this manner, one can freely use the abilities in present life for developing further excellence in these areas and enrich one's life.

Then one can work in these areas or fields of excellence. As one starts working, one develops the excellence in that area so easily that in no time one reaches the level of excellence where he was in last birth.

But these treasures too have dark lining. There is a hidden fear in the person to use these treasures to its full extent. Generally this happens because most of the times, a person has died while using these talents in the past life, so, using them to their fullest has a barrier, and so we have to work on that barrier in order to unfold the treasures to their fullest.

This is the reason why the moment we detect the presence of these treasures, we must check what had happened and how we had died while using these treasures.

We have already seen that only files that are open at death in our system are retained in the system, and if they are having some trauma, we have fears, but if they are not having a trauma, we need to find out how one had died in past life while using the talent. It helps us remove restraints connected with that death and we can use the talent to its fullest.

XL
Developing talents brought from past

It is seen that many times, one detects the talent, but still cannot use it to its fullest. This is because there is a fear deep down in the subconscious mind about the trauma attached with that talent. So one does not want to use it at all or use it to its fullest.

Once we detect these talents and find out why these talent files were left open in our system, we can proceed further. Then we can overcome the fear of using that talent to its fullest as now we become aware that whatever had happened, had happened in last birth and need not happen again now.

Once this subconscious restraint as well as inner fear goes away, the talent gets free and then we can use it to its fullest. So after we check the talent and find out the reason of death while we were using that talent in one of the past births, we can overcome all barriers and then achieve greater heights in success as far as that talent is considered.

When we start working on this talent, we do not start developing it from scratch or zero level, but we start from the point of mastery in it, where it was left in past life, so we are faster in developing it. Just as relearning of a thing takes much less time than first learning, learning of unfolded past talent takes less time to master it as compared to fresh learning.

DEATH BARRIER

- Death barrier

- Knowing & Feeling death barrier

- Problems while crossing death barrier

XLI

Death Barrier

Death Barrier is the point of death-experience that you have to cross to have an access to the memories in the past life.

This has to be done in presence of a master as one may find it difficult to handle some parts of this experience and may develop some acute problem as a result.

The stage of death barrier comes as you start remembering almost the event that had been experienced by you.

Why I said almost is because when you are reaching here, most of the times you feel you are imagining!

When your imagination is much closer to the reality and you almost remember the actual event that caused your death, you feel that as if the event is happening, you are actually dying.

You may feel the chocking and suffocation and breathless feeling for some seconds.

This is the time, the master has to be your side in the first time when you know & can handle this experience in future as you see your own past lives.

XLII

Knowing & feeling death barrier

When we are very close to the reality while imagining in the process of seeing past life, we start seeing something that we also start feeling intensely. This time, we feel we are actually going through the experience that we were initially imagining.

This is the time when we come very close to death barrier as we imagine death related event in story. May be this time, we feel like thinking something else very intensely as we start feeling suffocated or feel like death experience. This is the death barrier. A death barrier is an energy wall behind which many past life memories are stored and once we cross it, we get an access to them.

But if we try to cross it on our own, we get lot of inner resistance and most of the times, we cannot take this. Our mind gets diverted to some other better and comfortable imagination and we miss out this stage.

This is the time when we need a healer trainer's presence that can take us along this path and let us cross this death barrier.

Once the death barrier is detected, we need to cross it and once we do this, we are in the past life memories. Now we can access our past life memories, that store our past life traumas as well as treasures easily without experiencing death again.

XLIII

Problems while crossing death barrier

As we saw just now, in seeing past life, crossing death barrier is the most crucial stage. The greatest problem in it is the inner resistance that is made of fear of death. Fear of death comes not because we do not like death, but because experience of death has been very painful. This means, actually, fear of death is fear of pain during death.

If one tries to cross death barrier without expert help, one may get diverted constantly as one does not have inner strength to face the event that has cost life in one of the past lives.

Due to this, many efforts also lead a person to illusions of past, and not actual past life memories. Then one keeps imagining that one was Mr. X or Ms. Y (some powerful well-known figures in the past) in past life, but then actual access to powers of this X Y is lacking, as this is one's imagination & not the truth.

Such comfortable illusion is good to lure one's own mind, but that never takes us close to reality. People live in such illusions and keep telling others about them, but still, in one's own core one knows that they are illusions and so, one resists the hard path of crossing death barrier with search into past life traumas and phobias that one has carried due to them! If you want to see your true past life, you must learn to overcome this resistance.

SEEING PAST LIFE ON CROSSING DEATH BARRIER

- Seeing past life on crossing death barrier

- Vision of past life on crossing death barrier

- Future ability to see your other past lives alone

XLIV

Seeing past life on crossing death barrier

Once we cross the death barrier, we can remember things stored in our memory about past life very easily. Then seeing a past life is as easy as opening a container and taking things out of it. With this ability then one can remember any event from past life memory as and when one wants just by a process of simple remembering.

Our vision becomes clear and we can see what happened at a certain time and how we had reacted to it. Then we know the mistakes committed in past life and we can easily take care not to repeat them in this life. We can also learn to keep the past into past and keep the memories of it away from disturbing us in our present life.

This means, on seeing the past after crossing out death barrier, our overall vision gets clear and out thinking becomes more organised. We then know that our present problems are most of the times due to our entanglements in past memories, fears and confusions. Naturally, when the past threads are out, the present is free to create the future in its own way.

Every time later when we encounter some unknown feeling, we can sit and find out our past life related to that feeling and clear it so that it never comes again.

XLV

Vision of past life on crossing death barrier

When we are remembering the past, with the help of a trainer, as we cross the death barrier, we see what had happened and how we had died due to that. We also experience our death at this time, so this transition is known as a death barrier. As we cross this death barrier, we can see things as clearly as we remember things from our past in this life.

We all know how we remember things in our childhood. We certainly do not GO into our childhood when we remember it. In the same way, even here, we do not GO into our past, so COMING OUT of it is no problem at all.

Here, we can see details including the time, place, our past life name and age at which that event happened and names of others around us and so on.

But I suggest to see the details minus details that show your identity like name religion, nationality etc especially if you happen to find that you were some celebrity.

This is because if you are an ordinary person here right now, you may find yourself thinking about that life unnecessarily for longer duration and that will not be a good idea.

But for sure, if one wants one can get all these details once vision gets clear.

XLVI

Future ability to see your other past lives alone

Once we cross the death barrier and see your past in the presence of a healer, we can see our past life for ourselves any time.

Then, as and when we have time, we may sit in peace and unfold the pages of past for ourselves, following the same method that the healer had used for us.

This ability stays with all our life and even if we have a gap of several years, after that gap too if we wish, we can see our own past life whenever we feel like.

This means, whenever we feel that some emotions we are feeling have no relevance to our conscious and subconscious memories, we can search their roots in our past and handle them effectively.

Also, at times, we may find some past life treasures in the form of hidden abilities that may be accessible to us in this process.

Then as we have seen earlier, we may remove the burdens of resistance that are attached to the talent by further inner search and start using it further.

If we want, we may take support of other past life healing practitioners when we are seeing our further past lives, but ideally, if we do it ourselves, it is much better as then we can get greater insights as we need not share any thought with anyone, se we see freely.

NEED OF A MASTER TO CROSS DEATH BARRIER

- Need of a Master to cross death barrier
- Need of master to cross death barrier
- Effects of trying this without a master
- Risks in trying to see past life just by reading book
- What happens after crossing death barrier

XLVII

Need of a Master to cross death barrier

The whole thing here appears so easy and simple that one may feel that one can do this on one's own. But doing this without support for the first time is risky. Later support is not needed.

In fact while crossing the death barrier, one actually feels the death and experiences death while doing it for the first time. There is a choking sensation as well as suffocation and sinking feeling at times when one starts crossing death barrier. Some time, some people start crying uncontrollably and some feel a stabbing pain in some part of the body.

Due to this type of experiences, if a person tries to go to past life without a master around, one may have difficulties and then he may keep carrying all those feelings as problems for a long time.

At this time, if the master is present, he can take care of these things and helps a person to sail through this phase well without difficulty. So, I insist that for the first time, one has to get into past life only with a properly qualified and experienced master; as he knows when to stop you and when to heal you. He will never let you cross the death barrier hastily and will mellow down intensity of your experience.

Just as said above, a teacher is needed to be present with a person who is crossing the death barrier for the first time. This is because while crossing it for the first time, he actually undergoes death experience to some extent and a master dilutes the intensity of it as this can be very bad for some people. If the teacher is not present and if the trauma is not healed; the memory stays longer and person may develop headache or other problem after doing this stunt on his own. But the past life healing teacher heals the relevant trauma as soon as the seeker is feeling it and crossing it. As a result, a student who is seeing his past life for the first time has no problems later.

The presence of past life healing teacher can be in person or over internet chat or phone as is convenient for student and teacher, but in any way, while crossing death barrier for the first time, teacher has to be there. What a teacher does to heal this trauma differs from person to person. At times he has to use Reiki symbols while other times, he may have to clean the energies from chakras. This is because every person is unique and has a unique memory stored in his self about past.

Know that remembering trauma is always bad and more while entering past life; but trauma is an easiest gate to past, so we use it.

XLVIII
Effects of trying this without master

If anyone tries to go into the past life without the help of a qualified and experienced trainer for the first time, one may not be handle the experience of the death barrier. Then as the death barrier starts nearing, one may start deviating from the memory and start creating some stories that is comfortable.

By this one feels that one has seen something and experienced something, but it is just an imagination. If we wish to see the past, it is a good idea to see the actual past and not the virtual and imaginary one.

The test of real past vision is that the present life issue about which vision is related gets dissolved after the vision. But in case of the imaginations this never happens. We then imagine some other story to say that the issue is not getting clear due to this other issue.

But one thing is certain that it is very much difficult to get into real past life without a proper master; yet there are exceptions to any rule relating to such sciences. There are gifted people with spiritual inclination. They can see their past life just by wishing to see it. They do not need any method. But this is never the case with anyone and everyone.

Moreover, when a person wants to try it just by reading the book or so, he is certainly overconfident and may make mistakes.

When death barrier is closer, one may also get trapped in the feelings of death and then, as some start crying at the sight of the tragic death of their past life character, they also experience some pain that had produced their death in that life. But as the master is not there to help them in handling the pain, they develop actual pain and keep carrying it for long time. Eventually, such a pain may also develop into some major ailment.

This pain may be headache, body ache, joint pain, heart pain or anything like that. But the pain has no resembling physical symptoms. All the medical tests of such person are normal and then one keeps wondering about reasons of this type of pain or problem.

When one sees the past in the presence of a master while crossing death barrier, the master takes care of this type of pain and heals it there and then. This is the reason why a past life healing master has to be a master of many healing sciences as well.

I know of some one who had tried seeing past just by hearing about the method of seeing past life without hypnosis. The person managed to see something, but after that the person developed a very bad headache. He was not able to handle it in spite of many tests and medications. At the end, only after the person approached the past life healer, the healer was able to help him overcome the headache. So, please don't try this on your own for first time.

XLIX

Risks in trying to see past life just by reading book

This means, if you try to see your past life just by reading this book, you may have experiences similar to the person about whom I have said just now. So, be careful.

Never try getting into past life without a right teacher qualified to take others into past life. If someone says that he has learned past life, because he has done past life healing course, and so with the help of the book, he can take you into past life, be careful, as such a person may put you into a soup like the person I have described earlier.

These clear words of caution are needed because there are a few cases where people get into some things like that with the help of people with no knowledge or with half baked knowledge, or without any help at all.

But certain areas of this journey have slippery ways, so they need caution as well as support of the right person. In the absence of that one may get the same injuries that one had got in past life and again, if these injuries of past life are not healed in time, one may face the same consequences again.

But if one crosses these slippery ways with right guidance & support, one can not only heal the past life injuries; but can also release blocks they have created in our present life; & end the possibility of repetition of that event.

L
What happens after crossing death barrier

Once we cross death barrier, the gates of past open. Then we can get into past memories as and when we want and we know about this death experience so, it is not as dreadful as it was earlier. Also, after experiencing it once, the intensity of further experiences reduces and one has no problems later.

Here, when one is remembering the past experience, actually as we saw earlier, we start creating a story. Later we experience it. Then we feel that it is something that is happening with us, and slowly from our imagination, we slip into memory. It is the teacher who leads us into this memory for the first time with his leading questions.

Then, as we know the leading question types, we can ask them to our self and get into our past whenever we have the time and desire to see any past event related to anything in present. Once this happens, we can handle stumbling blocks from our present and access many hidden skills that we carry from our past.

This means, once we cross the death barrier, we can go on seeing many other past lives without the help of the master and then we can find that problems in our present life have started reducing as we remove past entanglements of attachments, confusions and fears from our present.

PAST LIFE VISION V/S IMAGINING & VISUALIZING

- Past life vision v/s imagining & visualizing

  - Imagination

  - Visualization

  - Creative visualization

- Imagination & Visualization

- Vision of past life memory

LI

Past life vision v/s imagining & visualizing

Though we follow a method of story creating and imagining while seeing past life, we can never forget the marked difference between imagination and vision.

In imagining, we are wildly thinking, whereas in Vision, we experience what we are seeing as if that event is something happening in the material reality around us.

When we are imagining and making a story on something in the presence of a master who is asking us leading questions, we start entering into the area where vision starts & imagination gets transformed into vision. There is a very subtle line between vision & imagination.

In imagination, we do not experience what we think of while, in vision, we see it as if we are experiencing it.

If we are following any other method of seeing past life, we may or may not be so sure of vision when we start seeing our past and we may end up in taking imagination as vision.

LII
Imagination

Imagination is the ability of forming mental images, sensations and concepts, in a moment when they are not perceived through sight, hearing or other senses. Imagination is the work of mind that helps us create things mentally. Imagination helps us to provide meaning to experience and understanding to knowledge. It is a fundamental facility through which people understand the world.

This is how imagination is technically defined. Everyone imagines some or the other thing at some point of time as per the need of the time or fancy of the mind.

Some imaginations stay as imaginations and become stories, while some imaginations are taken to be true over a period of time and then are taken to be reality.

Though I am not an atheist, I know that even God is an imagination of some people in the past that over a period of time is now taken to be reality. Images of God from every religion, place, community & time are different and are a result of the imagination of some group heads of that community or religion.

In the same way, at times, we imagine some thing happening to us and then take it to be true. But our subconscious mind knows that it is cooked up story. People use such stories for our benefit in life at times. And we too start with imagination in our journey to past, but we learn where to drop this imagination.

LIII
Visualization

The **classical** definition of visualization is as follows: the formation of mental visual images, the act or process of interpreting in visual terms or of putting into visual form. A **new** definition is a tool or method for interpreting image data fed into a computer and for generating images from complex multi-dimensional data sets.

Visualization is an old term which has received a large amount of interest in the computer science community. Visualization has previously been defined as the formation of visual images; the act or process of interpreting in visual terms or of putting into visual form.

More recently a new definition has been added: A tool or method for interpreting image data fed into a computer and for generating images from complex multi-dimensional data sets.

Another definition presented at a NASA internet site defines *datavisualization* as "exploring large amounts of raw data visually through the use of image processing and computer graphics in order to gain **understanding and insight** into the data."

In short visualization is seeing something mentally. We interpret things seen physically. This is seeing, but when we create mental images of things, it is called visualization. We all keep doing it but hardly know that it is visualization. We even use it in creating future with or without knowing.

LIV
Imagination & Visualization

When we imagine things, we have all the freedom to think of anything in the world. But, we cannot forget that every person imagines different events over the same situation. This is because imagination has a backing of vision.

One imagines things that he has known either in this life or past life, by experience of by watching experiences of others or by hearing stories of others. Event that has never experienced, heard, or seen is never imagined.

Very few people are aware of this fact behind imagination. The method of seeing past life without hypnosis taps exactly this fact that is hardly known. But unfortunately we find that many people get so much closed as they grow up that they even forget to imagine. They feel that they cannot imagine or create stories as telling stories or making stories is childish.

Then it becomes necessary to make them remember their childhood that makes them free to think like a child; then slowly lead them to imagination. Simple imagination is certainly baseless if it involves day dreaming, but the imagination needed for seeing past life is much different than this kind of daydreaming.

Yet, at times daydreams become the base thought of such an imagination and when the teacher asks leading questions, this day dreaming gets converted into some experience that one has forgotten due to lapse of a life.

LV
Vision of past life memory

When we enter the realm of vision from that of imagination with the help of leading questions of the teacher, one can actually have vision of past life. This vision actually becomes so clear that one knows it is no imagination.

When we imagine, we do not see things with details and feel the presence of these things with our eyes open. But when a person is having vision of past life memory, even if our eyes are wide open, we can see the events we are thinking we are imagining, actually happening in front of us. Then a point comes when something that is happening to the character we imagine in our story, is felt as our own experience. Generally this happens when we are just approaching the death barrier.

Then suddenly some details of the character that we actually are, change and we can start seeing some different details and that too as if from some place much above ground level, and we find that we cannot come down to the ground level even if we try hard. This is the point of our death in our past life.

Once we are clear of it in the presence of a teacher, we know how to go into our next past lives and how to differentiate imagination and vision of past life, and how to handle the trauma of past life when detected.

Then the way becomes like a cakewalk and we can go to any number of past lives.

GETTING CLARITY IN YOUR VISION

- Getting clarity in your vision
- Beginning to see
- Seeing and imagining
- Imagination free seeing
- Discarding imaginations
- Clarifying our own vision

LVI

Getting Clarity in your Vision

When you are seeing your own past lives in future, you need to have readiness to face the trauma and clarity of vision in order to understand clearly what you see.

Most of the times, due to absence of this readiness, one starts imagining, creating some stories and blurring the real vision one is getting.

This just keeps delaying the actual vision, as a result, your master needs much more time to take you in past and help you cross the death barrier.

Once one death barrier is crossed under supervision, later you can see as many past lives as possible on your own without anybody's help.

But of course, this does not give a peron the ability to take others into past life, as to help another person cross death barrier, one has to develop a tremendous level of positive energy, and also must have proper training to ask necessary questions and help a person sail through his past life safely.

Also, even after seeing the past life for the first time, in order to see future lives with least obsticles in your vision, the exercises given below are certainly going to be helpful.

To get the required clearly of vision you must remember a few things as you start seeing your past life.

1. When you start the process of imagining do not restrict yourself in anyway.
2. Do not bring any logic or similar theory when the imagination is on.

3. Even if you feel that what you are seeing is next to impossible, continue the process of imagining.
4. In this process, a point may come when one actually starts feeling the emotions and other feelings of some character in the vision.
5. When this starts, pay more attention on the details that you see.
6. Appearance, age, dress, name, names of other people, place, time of the day, year, names of different places you visit in this story/vision are some of the details you need to concentrate.
7. Never get attached to any character from your vision. Just watch and leave.

On following these thumb rules you can see past life with minimum difficulty. Then you can also see as many lives as possible with practice. But remember, the first time when you try this, you must not do it on your own or in the guidance of a novice. You must cross the death barrier only in the presence of a master.

LVII
Beginning to see

As we saw earlier, we start seeing past life with the help of imagination. Here we start with creating story suggested by our teacher. This sounds funny and childish to some, in the beginning, but teacher still asks a person to go ahead till one actually gets into past life vision.

The first vision is just a small glimpse that one sees for some time. As a result, it is quite unclear, but it is opening into a new path. This first step in past life is as important as the first step we take when we start walking.

When we begin to see, we must see the past life related to many more issues on one's own again and again. Then one must see if the issues related to them are dissolved or not.

If the issue is not dissolved, we must know that we have made a mistake in seeing past and what we claimed to see was just our imagination. Then we must sit all over again for seeing past life related to that issue.

When we repeat this for many instances, we start seeing our past with less difficulty and less mistakes. Yet, when we begin to see, there is tendency to identify our self with some hero we adore in this life.

This happens when we succumb to the attraction of finding out the name of the character we feel we are. Then we start thinking that we were that person in our past life. This may create problems in vision and its clarity, so, we must refrain from it.

LVIII
Seeing and imagining

Seeing and imagining are two different things. While seeing, we actually remember the past experiences, while in imagining, we are creating some story out of nothing.

Our process of seeing the past life begins with imagining and ends at seeing. But if this process is not handled well and if the seeker develops attachment to the imagination, this process may start with imagining and end at imagining. So, one has to be careful.

We see things that are in front of us, and in virtual seeing, we see events that are stored in memory. Both of these types of seeing have a good value as far as relevance to our life are concerned. Dreams contain virtual reality of our past experiences or present fears. So we say that we saw the dream.

Dreams belong to the category of seeing. But daydreaming belongs to the category of imagining. Similarly, making stories based on our desires, dreams, fears or phobias is called imagination. So imagination cannot be called seeing in any way whatsoever.

When we imagine, we never experience emotions related to the event we imagine, but, while we see any event, we experience these emotions. This is the major difference between seeing and imagining.

Whenever we start past life story making exercise, we must keep this factor in mind.

LIX

Imagination free seeing

Once we gain enough practice of imagining and then switching over to seeing, we do not need the ladder of Imagination. This happens when we have seen many past lives.

In case of some other situations where people suddenly see some things happening and those things happen in future, such things seen are called premonitions and fall in this category of seeing without imagination.

Many people get premonitions, but very few can understand that them as premonitions. They think that it is their fear that comes true or some start believing that some superpower tells them what is going to happen and so on.

Anyways, that is a totally different topic so we will not discuss it here, but we can say that as we go on seeing more and more past lives, we develop the ability to see the past without starting with imagination. As soon as we ask a question to ourselves as to why that particular fear or resistance is there, we start seeing the reason as the past life memory and soon that particular fear or resistance is out of our system. But this needs a lot of practice and many years of regular seeing of past lives.

Remember, we have a huge number of past lives but not all have traumas connected to them, so generally the ones that have traumas attached to them are seen in earlier visions and then we can even see regular ones.

LX

Discarding imaginations

When we are imagining and starting with the story for seeing past life, we must be aware every time that whatever we are creating is our imagination. This is necessary for keeping ourselves away from temptation of taking our imagination as vision.

Whenever we feel attachment to the character in our story as it is some historic character or some one much similar to what we are today, and then when we start feeling the experiences of that character, we must check if it is our imagination that is stretched too far.

Then we need to discard that imagination and that story, as we are attached to it, and start on different lines. This check keeps us away from imaginations that later can become past life illusions. Past life illusion is something which many take as past life vision.

Then they enjoy narrating that story of past life, but find that they are not progressing in present life with it. Therefore, such so called visions are to be called imaginations that we enjoy. We must discard them as imaginations.

This means, though imagination is the first step in seeing the past life, we must know where and how to discard the imagination and get into seeing. If one tries the experiment of getting into past life on his own and has never had any able guidance earlier, one may find it difficult to discard imaginations at right time.

LXI

Clarifying our own vision

While having vision we need to clarify it. As seen above, we must stop at a point while checking details. Especially, when you feel like naming some character that you imagine as the historic character you love. This is likely to make you feel inflated. But you must know that such a story is just YOUR imagination. Push away temptation to identify yourself with some historic character.

Of course, I am not saying that no hero of past will be born as an ordinary person in this birth, but we must always remember that all the qualities that distinguished him in the past life will also distinguish him in this birth and those qualities will be seen by others. So if you suspect that you were that, just work to develop qualities that your favourite hero had, so that you are recognised better.

Putting a check on our temptations to identify and imagine things we want is the greatest key to clarify our vision. While seeing past life, we must be as ruthless to our inner self as possible. This is because, here, inner self is at its best playing games with conscious self. It shows things that it wants to see, and at times makes conscious self believe it.

When you are seeing past life for the first time, you will learn from your teacher how dangerous can this act of inner self be, for the clarity of your past life vision.

Once you know it, keep guarding temptations of inner self and keep seeing or imagining things that are just pure imagination and keep seeing things when you know it is a memory. Then keep seeing as many details as you can see, and check the authenticity of each detail on the basis of experience.

Remember, even when we have started by imagining and creating a story, the story we have created is a pathway that takes us into real memories. Imagination has loose ends and ambiguities, but reality never has them. So when you are about to experience the things and events from the story you are making, start checking for details and start closing the ends so that imagination gets dropped and your vision gets cleared.

At such times, suddenly, you may find that the face or some details of the character you were imagining till now are different. It is fine at such times, you must continue as this happens as your vision gets cleared.

Perfect clarity of vision may be achieved after many repetitions of seeing past life, but every time, we need to keep clearing the vision as we move from our imagination to memories.

If we do not do this, we may end up in calling imagination as vision as we have seen earlier. So this exercise of clearing vision is necessary and we must start it as soon as we start feeling some inner pull while we are in the process of creating the story.

APPENDIX

- Tips and cautions of past life healing
- Creating powerful future after healing past lives

LXII

Creative visualization

Creative visualization is a mental technique that uses the imagination to make dreams come true. Used in the right way, creative visualization can improve our life. It also helps us to attract success and prosperity. It is a power that can alter our environment, circumstances that make events happen, attract money, possessions, work, people or love in life. Creative visualization uses the power of mind. It is the power behind every success.

By visualizing a certain event, situation or an object, we attract it into our life. It is similar to daydreaming. To some it may appear as magic, but there is no magic involved. It is natural process of natural mental laws known as power of thought.

There are people who use this technique naturally in their everyday affairs, not being aware that they are using some sort of power. All successful people use it knowingly or unknowingly, attracting the success they want into their life, by visualizing their goals as already accomplished.

The power of visualization is a mighty power, but there are some limits to using it. These limits are within us, not in the power. We often limit ourselves and cannot look beyond a limited circle. We limit ourselves by our thoughts and beliefs. The more open-minded we can be, and the more bigly we dare to think, the greater are our opportunities and possibilities. Limitations are within our minds, and it is up to us to rise above them.

LXIII

Tips and cautions in past life healing

Now you must have realised how important it is to see the past life and how careful one has to be while seeing it. So here are some tips for seeing past life for second time onwards, as you know that first time has to be in the presence of a master; and for using it powerfully in this life.

Seeing past life is very useful in making our present life better, but here we also need to have many precautions.

Many people just want to see past life out of curiosity and let anyone see their past life, just because that person says that he or she can see the past life of others.

But remember, your past life is your own personal thing and you need to be very careful in letting anyone help you in seeing your past life. This is because; it may also be very dangerous if you are in wrong hands.

Here are some precautions you need to take in seeing past life. Read them carefully before you choose a master to help you in letting you see your past life.

Firstly, you may find that some phobias are related to particular past event and such events repeatedly produce great hurdle in your growth.

You can heal these phobias with the help of past life vision. Also, we find that we attract some phobias.

At such times, we must remember that we like only the things that benefit us.

So, if you find yourself getting attached to some past life memory or to some trauma or phobia, you must try to find out what benefit you are trying to seek out of this act.

If you do this you may find something to which you are stuck. You may also find that you are seeking some benefit from that phobia.

But many a times it is observed that the moment you try to find out this benefit, some such thing happens that the attention gets diverted from the search to this thing that happens.

It may be just a physical pain or some other problem that you have to attend to immediately.

If this happens again and again, you must seek the support of the master.

He will help you come over it and help you to get rid of this feeling of stuck ness by releasing it.

Generally this may happen once or twice after you start seeing your own past lives. Then you will know how to handle this situation.

Second precaution is that you must not discuss the past life you are working on, on your own to those who do not know anything about past life vision by this method.

Even people who talk about past life regression are not the ones who know about this method of past life vision.

So, they may lead you in the wrong direction if they have no proper experience.

Thirdly, you need to be very careful of your subconscious pressures when you start working on past life.

This is because, the moment you get tensed, your attention is likely to get diverted from what you are seeing to what feel due to tension. This blurs your vision and you may not be able to continue to see clearly.

It may also happen that if you wish to see or avoid something and one getting tense, you may create the same vision out of your imagination which may not be the real past life vision. It may be just a mixed creation of your present life experience and your creative mind.

If this starts happening, you may start creating a number of unrealistic visions and may fall in the trap of considering them true and considering you as the super hero or heroine or the suffering hero or heroine which is false.

Remember this is just a defence mechanism of your conscious and sub-conscious mind of this life.

When mind is in a defensive state, it cannot move ahead in simple, cool and casual way as it is necessary to see the past life.

Fourthly, DO NOT develop an addition of Past Life vision by trying to relate practically every thing you get stuck at to your past life.

This could be an easy escape from seeing your errors and indirectly a refusal to correct them and get what you want. Remember, past life trauma generate involuntary actions to some situations but where you see if, the root cause automatically gets released and the reflex reaction to that kind of situation stops.

So past life cannot be a defence for present acts.

Past life memory may justify some reflexes if and only if they vanish after remembering the trauma.

If find that person is still having the same reflex and is justifying it with past life memory, be sure that, that past life memory is not real.

It is just a creation of one's own sub-conscious which he is using to cover his mistakes and shortcomings that one does not want to admit.

This kind of defence weakens your vision. So if you find yourself doing it stop it.

Fifthly, you must be open to admit your own faults gracefully.

This attitude will help you have a clearer vision and also get rid of the past traumas more easily.

Remember sometimes, the traumas that you had suffered from in your past life are due to your own mistakes.

You may keep doing the same mistake now too leading yourself in the similar situation. So, if you learn to accept and correct the mistakes, you may come out of this vicious circle.

If you remember these precautions and take them when you start working on your own past life, I am sure you will soon develop very good vision with the help of which you may be able to know, heal and handle many events in your past so that your present future becomes cleared these shocks and traumas.

Also you can get help from the skills you had developed in your past life. This may enrich your present life to a very great extent.

LXIV

Creating powerful future after healing past life

On healing past our lives the blocks that cause problems vanish. Now we lead a clearer life.

Once this is done, one can create future as one wants. This means, once past is clear; future is not a repetition of past life.

Now future becomes a clean slate and one can write whatever one wants on it.

Now we can dream about whatever we want to achieve and use creative visualization to bring our dreams to reality.

Now nothing can come in the way of our dreams. We can have a smooth life ahead.

Now there is no need to entertain any baseless fears.

But still in this stage, if any fear appears and if the fear does not seem to have any root in our memory, we are free to check the relevant past life and clear it.

We must never forget that we all have had many lives in past and we might remember only a few out of them. So there is still a chance to carry some fears or obsessions.

When we start writing on the clean slate of our future, we may encounter some fears, thoughts or obsessions and then we may have to work on them again.

But we must take care while creating our future. We must never get excessively attached to any desire, person, or event; else we create problem for our future.

Check out for thoughts in sub-conscious. Remember that whenever our intention is not getting fulfilled, some resistance from our own sub-conscious is responsible for it.

There is a common tendency of blaming other people or past karmas or luck or circumstances for our failure, but once you clear your past, know that all such factors are fully cleared.

Now if you fail, the circumstances within mind, i.e. your own thoughts are responsible for that. So look out for inner resistance to any wish action or desire.

Work on it instead of wasting time and energy of blaming outside factors, gathering sympathy & enjoying failure.

If you catch sub-conscious resistance, work on it and then start working on our wish. If we do this we will never fail in our venture.

So we can say that the key to a perfect desired future has the following steps:

1. **Define your intention**
2. **Make details of intention clear to you**
3. **Complete the gaps in clarity**
4. **Think of possible obstacles**
5. **Check which of them are real**
6. **Work first on virtual obstacles**
7. **Then work on real obstacles**
8. **Check if all obstacles are clear**
9. **Now check again & redefine intention**
10. **Work to materialize your intention.**

If you follow these steps, you can create future of your choice after clearing the past.

Let us see how you can do this:

1. **Define your intention**

When you wish something in future, define your wish clearly. This means, know what exactly you want, when and how. Know your desire clearly, know if it is just a passing by wish, or dream or it is an actual desire that you want to come true in your life.

1. **Make details of intention clear to you**

Think of all possible details that you want in the event or place or person or thing you wish to have. Let these details be as accurate as you wish. This clears vision of the intention.

3. **Complete the gaps in clarity**

You may find some gaps in the intention in spite of clarifying vision. At such times, we must complete the gaps.

4. **Think of possible obstacles**

Think of possible obstacles that may come in the way of reaching your goal. These obstacles in your goal reaching or intention fulfilment may be either real ones due to your limits or shortcomings, or may be virtual originating from your inner fears of failures. You must work on these obstacles before you start working on your intention.

5. **Check which of them are real**

When you think of obstacles in the path of your goal, study them and find out which of the possible obstacles are real ones and which ones are just creations of your mind. This can happen only when you study the obstacles thoroughly and check the feelings you get near your naval when you think of obstacles.

6. **Work first on virtual obstacles**

Obstacles created by mind are virtual ones. They are seen due to our fears. Mostly after clearing the past, the only fear that stays is the learned fear of failure. So, first Work on mind for the obstacles created by your mind.

7. **Then work on real obstacles**

Once you handle your mind, work on real obstacles by improving yourself, removing your shortcomings in various areas and preparing yourself to reach the goal.

8. **Check if all obstacles are clear**

Check the situations again and see if all obstacles are clear or not. If anything is still left out, remove these left out obstacles too.

9. **Now check again & redefine intention**

Now check if in the new circumstances, you still have the originally defined intention or do you wish to change it or modify it. If so, change or modify your intention.

10. **Work to materialize your intention.**

When your intention is finally defined and when the path to your goal is clear; work on your intention and reach your destination.

When you follow above steps carefully and work on your intentions, you create future that you want and make it materialize the way in which you want it to materialize.

This is the reason why, when many people asked me if I can show them their future just as I help them see their past, I told them clearly that future is just a repetition of past and so, if the slate of past is clear, we can write anything that we want on that blank slate and create the future that we have always wanted to be in.

But remember this is a job of great responsibility as now whatever we wish and work to create will not be obstructed by any destiny or obstacles from past, so they will materialize more easily.